# The Miraculous Qur'an and Some of Its Mysteries

*from the Risale-i Nur Collection*
Humanity's Encounter with the Divine Series

# The Miraculous Qur'an and Some of Its Mysteries

- *The Twelfth Word*
- *The Twentieth Word*
- *The Twenty-fifth Word*
- *The Twenty-ninth Letter*

Bediüzzaman
SAİD NURSİ

New Jersey

Copyright © 2013 by Tughra Books
First edition published as *The Mysteries of the Qur'an* 2002
Revised Edition 2006
16 15 14 13    3 4 5 6

Published by Tughra Books
345 Clifton Ave., Clifton,
NJ, 07011, USA

www.tughrabooks.com

Translated from Turkish by Ali Ünal

Library of Congress Cataloging-in-Publication Data

Nursi, Said, 1877-1960.
  [Risale-i nur. English. Selections]
  The Mysteries of the Qur'an / Bediuzzaman Said Nursi.
     p. cm. --  (Humanity's encounter with the divine ; 7)
  "From the Risale-i Nur collection."
  Includes bibliographical references (p.     ) and index.
  ISBN 1-59784-004-1 (pbk. : alk. paper)  1. Nurculuk--Doctrines. 2.
Koran--Criticism, interpretation, etc.  I.
Title. II. Series.
BP252.R5713 2002
297.1'221--dc21

                                        2002013931

ISBN 978-1-59784-004-0

Printed by
Çağlayan A.Ş., Izmir - Turkey

# Table of Contents

## THE TWELFTH WORD

### Revealed Wisdom and
### Human Thought

[Differences between the Qur'anic wisdom and human philosophy • Moral training in one's personal life • Moral training in human social life • The Qur'an is superior to all other Divine Scriptures, speech, and writings]

## THE TWENTIETH WORD

### The Qur'an:
### Eloquence and Science

[Apparently insignificant events hide a universal principle and present the tip of a general law • The Prophets' miracles show what humanity can attain through observation, experimentation, and concerted effort]

## THE TWENTY-FIFTH WORD

### The Miraculous Qur'an

[Said Nursi's definition of the Qur'an ]

[An analysis of verses exhibiting the Qur'an's miraculous eloquence]

## THE TWENTY-NINTH LETTER

## The Qur'an

# Bediüzzaman and the Risale-i Nur

In the many dimensions of his lifetime of achievement, as well as in his personality and character, Bediüzzaman (1877-1960) was and, through his continuing influence, still is an important thinker and writer in the Muslim world. He represented in a most effective and profound way the intellectual, moral and spiritual strengths of Islam, evident in different degrees throughout its fourteen-century history. He lived for eighty-five years. He spent almost all of those years, overflowing with love and ardor for the cause of Islam, in a wise and measured activism based on sound reasoning and in the shade of the Qur'an and the Prophetic example.

Bediüzzaman lived in an age when materialism was at its peak and many crazed after communism, and the world was in great crisis. In that critical period, Bediüzzaman pointed people to the source of belief and inculcated in them a strong hope for a collective restoration. At a time when science and philosophy were used to mislead young generations into atheism, and nihilistic attitudes had a wide appeal, at a time when all this was done in the name of civilization, modernization and contemporary thinking and those who tried to resist them were subjected to the cruelest of persecutions, Bediüzzaman strove for the overall revival of a whole people, breathing into their minds whatever and spirits whatever is taught in the institutions of both modern and traditional education and of spiritual training.

Bediüzzaman had seen that modern unbelief originated from science and philosophy, not from ignorance as previously. He wrote that nature is the collection of Divine signs and therefore science and religion cannot be conflicting disciplines. Rather, they are two (apparently) different expressions of the same truth. Minds should be enlightened with sciences, while hearts need to be illumined by religion.

Bediüzzaman was not a writer in the usual sense of the word. He wrote his splendid work the *Risale-i Nur*, a collection exceeding 5,000 pages, because he had a mission: he struggled against the materialistic and atheistic trends of thought fed by science and philosophy and tried to present the truths of Islam to modern minds and hearts of every level of understanding. The *Risale-i Nur*, a modern commentary of the Qur'an, mainly concentrates on the existence and unity of God, the Resurrection, Prophethood, the Divine Scriptures primarily including the Qur'an, the invisible realms of existence, Divine Destiny and humanity's free will, worship, justice in human life, and humanity's place and duty among the creation.

In order to remove from people's minds and hearts the accumulated 'sediment' of false beliefs and conceptions and to purify them both intellectually and spiritually, Bediüzzaman writes forcefully and makes reiterations. He writes in neither an academic nor a didactic way; rather he appeals to feelings and aims to pour out his thoughts and ideas into people's hearts and minds in order to awaken them to belief and conviction.

This book is a selected section from the *Risale-i Nur* collection.

# Revealed Wisdom and Human Thought

In the Name of God,
the Merciful, the Compassionate.

Whoever has been given the Wisdom, certainly has been given much good. (2:269)

[Note: This Word presents a brief comparison between the Qur'an's sacred wisdom and human philosophy, a concise summary of the Qur'anic instruction and training for humanity's personal and social life, and an indication of the Qur'an's superiority to all other Divine Words and speech.]

## Four fundamentals

**FIRST FUNDAMENTAL:** Differences between the Qur'anic wisdom and human philosophy: A religious, skillful, and renowned ruler wanted to make a copy of the Qur'an as beautifully as required by its sacred meanings and miraculous wording in order to adorn its wonderful words in a worthy fashion. So, he wrote it in a truly wonderful fashion with all kinds of precious jewels. To point out the variety of its truths, he wrote some of its letters in diamonds and emeralds, others in pearls and agate, brilliants and coral, and gold and silver. He adorned and decorated in such a way that everyone was full of admiration and astonishment. That Qur'an became a most precious artwork for the people of truth, for its outer beauty indicated its brilliant inner beauty and striking adornment.

The ruler showed this Qur'an to a foreign [non-Muslim] philosopher and a Muslim scholar. Seeking to test and reward them, he told each one to write about it. The two men complied. The philosopher discussed the letters' shapes, decorations, and inter-relationships, and the jewels' properties and methods of use. He said nothing of its meaning, for he saw only an ornamented object and was unaware that it was an invaluable book with depths of meaning. As he was well-informed about engineering and chemistry, could describe things, and knew a great deal about jewelry but nothing about Arabic, he wrote his book accordingly. But the truth-loving Muslim scholar, understanding that it was the Clear Book (the Wise Qur'an), ignored its outward ornamentation and the letters' decorations and described the sacred truths and secret lights behind the veil of decorations, for they are far more valuable and worthy of respect, more useful and comprehensive.

Both men presented their books to the ruler, who began with the philosopher's book. Seeing that he had worked very hard, the ruler nevertheless refused his book and expelled him from his presence. Why? Because he had written nothing of the bejeweled Qur'an's true wisdom, understood none of its meanings, and showed his disrespect for it by thinking that this source of truths consists of meaningless decoration. Looking through second book, and seeing that the truth-loving scholar had written a very beautiful and useful interpretation, a wise and illuminating composition, he congratulated him. It was pure wisdom, and its author was a true scholar, a genuine sage. As a reward, the scholar was given 10 gold coins from the ruler's inexhaustible treasury for each letter of his book.

The meaning is as follows: The embellished Qur'an is this artistically fashioned universe; the ruler is the Eternal Sovereign. The first man represents the line of philosophy and philosophers; the second man represents the way of the Qur'an and its students. Indeed, the wise Qur'an is the most exalted expounder and a most eloquent translator of this universe (a macro-Qur'an). It is the Criterion that instructs jinn and humanity in the signs of creation—Divine laws regarding creation and the universe's operation—inscribed by the Pen of Power on the sheets of the universe and pages of time. It looks upon creatures, each a meaningful letter, as bearing the meaning of another (on account of their Maker) and says: "How beautifully they have been made, how meaningfully they point to the Maker's beauty and grace." Thus it shows the universe's real beauty.

Philosophy, focused on the design and decorations of creation's "letters," has lost its way. While it ought to look upon this macro-book's letters as bearing the meaning of another (on account of God), it looks upon them as signifying themselves (on account of themselves) and says: "How beautiful they are," not "How beautifully they have been made." Thus philosophers insult creation and cause it to complain. In truth, materialistic philosophy is a falsehood having no truth, an insult to creation.

***SECOND FUNDAMENTAL:*** Moral training in one's personal life: Sincere students of philosophy are Pharaoh-like tyrants.[1] They abuse themselves by bowing in worship before the meanest thing, if they perceive it to be in their interest to do so. These materialist students are stubborn, misleading, and unyielding, but so wretched that they accept endless degradation for one pleasure; unbending but so mean as to kiss the feet of devilish people for a base advantage. They are conceited and domineering, but, unable to find any point of support in their hearts, are utterly impotent and vainglorious tyrants. Such people are no more than self-centered egoists striving to gratify their material and carnal desires, pursuers of personal interests and certain national interests.

Sincere students of the Qur'an are worshipping servants of God. They do not degrade themselves by bowing in worship before even the greatest of the created. They are dignified servants who do not worship in order to obtain a benefit, even Paradise. They are modest students, mild and gentle, who only

---

[1] Pharaoh is a title given to the kings of ancient Egypt. This particular one lived during the time of Prophet Moses and was exceptionally arrogant and cruel. (Tr.)

lower themselves voluntarily to their Creator, never exceeding what He has permitted. They are aware of their weakness and need, but are independent because the Munificent Owner provides them with spiritual wealth. Relying on their Master's infinite Power, they are powerful. They act and strive purely for God's sake and pleasure, and to be equipped with virtue. The training given by philosophy and the Qur'an may be understood through the above comparison.

**THIRD FUNDAMENTAL:** Moral training in human social life: Philosophy considers force to be the point of support in social life, and life as the realization of self-interest (its goal) and conflict (its principle). A community's unifying bonds are race and aggressive nationalism, and its fruits are the gratification of carnal desires and increased need. Force calls for aggression, seeking self-interest causes battles over material resources, and conflict brings strife. Racism feeds by swallowing others, thereby paving the way for aggression. This is why humanity is not happy.

The Qur'an accepts right as the point of support in social life. The aim is virtue and God's approval, and its principle is mutual assistance. The only community bonds it accepts are those of religion, profession, and country. Its aim is to control and thus weaken carnal desires by urging the soul to sublime matters, satisfying our exalted feelings so that we will strive for human perfection and true humanity. Right calls for unity, virtues bring solidarity, and mutual assistance means helping each other. Religion secures brotherhood, sisterhood, and cohesion. Restraining our desires and urging the soul to perfection brings happiness in both worlds.

**FOURTH FUNDAMENTAL:** The Qur'an is superior to all other Divine Scriptures, speech, and writings: This truth is explained in the following two parables: First, a king has two forms of speech and address. He uses the first one while speaking on his phone to a common subject regarding a minor matter or private need. He uses the second one in his capacity as the supreme sovereign, supreme head of the religious office, and supreme ruler. He directs his words toward an envoys or high official so that his commands will be promulgated through an exalted decree that manifests his majesty.

Second, a person holds a mirror toward the sun. According to the mirror's capacity, he receives the sun's seven-colored light and thereby establishes a connection with it. When he directs this light-filled mirror toward his dark house and roof-covered garden, he benefits from the sun only according to the mirror's ability to reflect it. Another person opens broad windows in his house or roof-covered garden, thus exposing them to the benefits of direct and continuous sunlight. In gratitude, he says: "O fine sun, beauty of the world and skies, who gilds Earth with your light and makes flowers smile. You have furnished my house and garden with your heat and light, just as you have done for the skies, Earth, and flowers." The first person cannot say such things, for he has to be content with his mirror's reflections of the sun's light and heat.

Consider the Qur'an in the light of these two parables. See its miraculousness and understand its holiness. The Qur'an declares: If all the trees on Earth were to become pens and all the seas ink, and if they were to write the words of Almighty God, they would never finish them.

The Qur'an holds the greatest rank among God's infinite words because it originated in His Greatest Name and in the greatest level of every Name, each of which has infinitely different levels of manifestation.[2] It is the Word of God because He is the Lord of the Worlds; His decree because He is the Deity of all creatures; and a Divine address because He is the Creator of the Heavens and Earth. It is a speech of God in regard to His absolute Lordship, an eternal address in regard to His universal Divine Sovereignty; a ledger of the All-Merciful One's favors from the point of view of His all-embracing, comprehensive Mercy; a collection of communications that sometimes begin with ciphers in respect of His Divinity's sublime majesty; and a wisdom-infusing Holy Scripture that, having originated from the Divine Greatest Name's all-comprehensive realm, looks to and examines the all-embracing domain of the Supreme Throne of God. This is why the Qur'an deserves to be called— and is called—the Word of God.

Some other Divine Words are Divine speech manifested for a specific reason, under a minor title, and through the particular manifestation of a particular Name. This results from a particular man-

---

[2] For example, the manifestations of the All-Coloring and the All-Decorating in spring are not at the same level as in winter. (Tr.)

ifestation of Divine Lordship, Sovereignty, or Mercy. Divine Words vary in degree with respect to particularity and universality. Most inspiration is of this kind. For example, in ascending order, God sends the most particular and simple inspiration to animals. It increases in importance as it is sent to ordinary people, ordinary angels, saints, and greater angels, respectively.

This is why saints who supplicate without mediation directly through the telephone of the heart "connected to God" say: "My heart reports to me from my Lord." They do not say: "It reports to me from the Lord of the Worlds." They can say: "My heart is a mirror, a Throne, of my Lord," but not: "My heart is the Throne of the Lord of the Worlds," for saints receive the Divine address only according to their capacity and to how many of the 70,000 veils separating humanity and God they have removed.

A king's decree issued in his capacity as the supreme sovereign is higher and more exalted than his conversation with a commoner. We receive far more benefit from direct exposure to the sun than we do from its reflection. The Qur'an is superior to all speech and books in the same way. Next come the other Divine Scriptures,[3] which are superior to all other speech and books, for they are based on Revelation. If all non-Qur'anic but nevertheless fine words, epigrams, and wise sayings known to humanity and jinn were collected, they could not equal the Qur'an.

If you want to have some understanding of how the Qur'an has originated in God's Greatest Name and in the greatest level of every Name, consider the universal, sublime statements of *Ayat al-Kursi* (2:255) and the following verses:

> God, there is no god but He; the Ever-Living, the Self-Subsisting (by Whom all subsist.) Slumber seizes Him not, nor sleep. To Him belongs all that is in the heavens and all that is in the earth. Who is there that shall intercede with Him save by His leave? He knows what lies before them and what lies after them, (what lies in their future and in their past, what is known to them and what is hidden from them;) and they comprehend not anything of His Knowledge save what He wills. His Seat (of dominion) embraces the heavens and Earth, and their preservation wearies Him not; He is the All-High, the Tremendous. (2:255)

> With Him are the keys of the Unseen. (6:59)

_____

[3] Divine Books and Pages.

O God, Owner of sovereignty. (3:26)

He covers the day with the night, each pursuing the other urgently. (7:54)

O Earth, swallow your water, and O sky, cease your rain! (11:44)

The seven heavens and Earth, and all within them extol Him. (17:44)

Your creation and your upraising are as but as a single soul. (31:28)

We offered the Trust to the heavens and Earth and the mountains. (33:72)

On the day when We shall roll up heaven as a scroll is rolled for books. (21:104)

They measure not God as is due to Him. Earth altogether shall be His handful on the Day of Resurrection. (39:67)

If We had sent down this Qur'an upon a mountain, you would have seen it humbled, split asunder out of the fear of God. (59:21)

Meditate upon the initial verses of those *suras* beginning with *al-hamdu li-llah* (All praise be to God) or *tusabbihu* (glorifies Him), and try to understand this significant fact. Look at the openings of those *sura*s beginning with *Alif Lam Mim, Alif Lam Ra,* and *Ha Mim*, and try to understand the Qur'an's importance in God Almighty's sight.

If you understand the significant kernel of this fourth fundamental, you understand the following facts:

- Revelation mostly came to Prophets via an angel; inspiration is mostly without mediation.

- The greatest saint cannot attain the level of any Prophet.

- The Qur'an possesses its own grandeur, sacred glory and honor, which are the sources of its sublime miraculousness.

- Prophet Muhammad was honored with Ascension, ascended to the Heavens, reached the furthest lote-tree and to the distance of only *two bows' length*,[4] and there supplicated the All-Majestic One, Who is closer to us than our jugular veins, and returned in the twinkling of an

---

[4] The furthest lote-tree signifies the furthest limit to which a mortal, however great, can reach. The distance of two bows' length signifies the nearness Prophet Muhammad attained in the Ascension to the Almighty, which is unattainable by any other mortal. (Tr.)

eye for specific reasons. Just as splitting the moon was a miracle of Messengership demonstrating his Prophethood to the jinn and humanity, the Ascension was a miracle of his worship and servanthood to God demonstrating to spirits and angels that he is the Beloved of God.

O God, bestow blessings and peace upon him and his Family[5] as befits Your Mercy and his dignity.

---

[5] The Prophet's Family: The Prophet, Ali, Fatima, Hasan, and Husayn are known as the *Ahl al-Bayt*, the Family (or People) of the House. The Prophet's wives are not included here.

# The Qur'an: Eloquence and Science

**Two stations**

In the Name of God,
the Merciful the Compassionate.

**FIRST STATION:** Consider the following verses:

When We said unto the angels: "Prostrate before Adam," they fell prostrate, all save Iblis. (2:34)

God commands you to sacrifice a cow. (2:67)

Yet after all this your hearts were hardened and become like rocks or even harder. (2:74)

Once, Satan suggested three things about these verses:

You say that the Qur'an is a miracle of infinite eloquence and guidance for everyone forever. So why does it persistently repeat, in a sort of historical manner, certain insignificant events like slaughtering a cow and even naming the longest sura (al-Baqara means "The Cow") after that event? Also, the angels' prostrating before Adam is a matter of the Unseen and reason cannot comprehend it. It may be accepted and affirmed only after one has attained a strong belief, and yet the Qur'an addresses all those who have reason or intellect and frequently warns: 'Will they not use their reason?' Additionally, what kind of guidance is intended by describing so forcefully certain natural conditions of rocks that are only results of chance?

The following points occurred to me.

*FIRST POINT:* The Qur'an contains many apparently insignificant events, each of which hides a universal principle and present the tip of a general law. For example: *(He) taught Adam the names of all of them* (2:31) states that Adam was taught "the names" as a miracle to show his superiority over the angels in being favored with God's vicegerency on Earth—the rule of Earth in the name of God.

Although this seems a small and particular event, it constitutes a tip of the following universal principle: Due to Adam's comprehensive nature, humanity was taught (or given the potential to obtain) a great deal of information, many sciences concerning all aspects of the universe, and vast knowledge about the Creator's Attributes and acts. All of this made humanity superior to the angels, the heavens, Earth, and the mountains, for only humanity could bear the Supreme Trust. It also made humanity Earth's ruler in God's name.

Likewise, the angels' prostration before Adam, in contrast with Satan's rejection, is a small, particular event in the Unseen. However, it is the tip of a most comprehensive and universally observed principle and suggests a most extensive truth: By mentioning their obedience and submission and Satan's haughty refusal, the Qur'an shows that most material beings in the universe and their spiritual representatives are subjugated to us and ever-ready to satisfy our needs and desires.

In addition, the Qur'an warns us about evil beings and their immaterial representatives, as well as Earth's devilish inhabitants who corrupt our potential for perfection and seduce us into wrong paths. It reminds us of these terrible enemies and great obstacles we will encounter on the path of progress toward perfection. Thus, while narrating a particular event pertaining to a single individual (Adam) the Qur'an of Miraculous Expression holds an elevated discourse with all creation and humanity.

*SECOND POINT:* Although part of the Sahara desert, the blessed Nile's bounteous gifts have made Egypt a fertile, arable land. Such a blessed, paradise-like land being adjacent to the hellish Sahara caused farming and agriculture to be so established in the Egyptians' very nature that agriculture became sanctified and cows and bulls became objects of worship. In fact, the Egyptians of Moses' time worshipped cows and bulls, as can be seen by the Jews making a calf to worship years after the Exodus. The Qur'an explains that Moses, by sacrificing a cow and through his Messengership, eradicated this ingrained concept. Thus this apparently insignificant event points to a universal principle with an elevated miraculousness, and expounds upon it as a most essential lesson of wisdom for everyone at all times.

By analogy, certain minor incidents mentioned in the Qur'an as historical events are tips of universal principles. In *Lema'at*, in the "Treatise of the Miraculousness of the Qur'an," I used, as examples, the seven sentences of Moses' story to explain how each part of those particular sentences contains a significant universal principle.

*THIRD POINT:* Consider the following verse:

> Yet after all this your hearts were hardened and became like rocks, or even harder: For there are rocks from which rivers gush, and some from which, when they are cleft, water issues; and some which fall down for awe of God. God is not unaware of what you do. (2:74)

While reciting this verse, Satan asked: "Why are certain natural conditions of rocks, known to everyone, mentioned as if they were among the most important issues?" In response, the following point issued from the Qur'an's enlightenment: It is appropriate to do so, and there is a need for it, for only through the Qur'an's miraculous conciseness and bounty of enlightenment has the matter been simplified and summarized.

Conciseness is a foundation of the Qur'an's miraculousness, and bountiful enlightenment and beauty of explanation are parts of its guidance. These qualities require that universal truths and profound yet general principles be presented in simple terms to the broad masses that make up the majority of the Qur'an's audience. As most people are not deep thinkers, it requires that only their tips and simple forms should be shown. Also all events, each a Divine operation whose extraordinary character is veiled by familiarity, should be pointed out briefly.

Thus, because of this subtle reality, this verse says:

> O Children of Israel and children of Adam, why have your hearts become harder and more lifeless than rocks? Look at those very hard, lifeless, large rocks formed in vast underground strata. See how obedient and submissive they are to Divine commands, how permeable and open they are to His Lordship's acts. This is so clear that the ease with which the Divine operations form trees can be seen with the same ease, order, and perfect wisdom underground. Water flows to them without resistance, just like blood circulating in veins, in well-arranged water channels and veins through hard, deaf rocks.[6]

---

[6] It is only fitting that the Qur'an should explain the three important tasks that the Majestic Creator entrusted to rock strata, the foundation of the magnificent, moving palace that we call Earth. The first task: Just as Earth acts, by the Lord's Power, as a "mother" to plants and raises them, so by the Divine Power do the rocks act as a "nurse" to Earth and "raise" it. The second task: They serve the orderly circulation of water in Earth's body, like the circulation of blood [in our bodies]. The third task: They act as a "treasurer" to the appearance and

Just as tree and plant branches spread easily, the roots' delicate veins spread underground with the same ease and lack of resistance from rocks.

The Qur'an points to this and teaches a comprehensive truth through that verse, and so by allusion says to the hard-hearted:

O Children of Israel and children of Adam. You are weak and impotent, and yet you can make your hearts so hard that they resist the Divine Being's commands. Huge strata of hard rocks perform their subtle tasks perfectly in darkness and in total submission to His commands. They act as a source of water and other means of life for all living creatures in such a way, and as means for their division and distribution with such wisdom and justice, that they are as malleable as wax or even air in the hand of Power of the All-Wise One of Majesty. Without resistance, they prostrate before His Power's vastness, for almost the same well-arranged occurrences and wise and gracious Divine operations that we see above ground take place underground.

_____

continuation, with well-ordered balance, of springs and rivers, sources and streams. Rocks "write" and scatter over Earth's face "evidences" of Divine Unity that they cause to flow, with all their strength, in "mouthfuls" in the form of water, which serves life.

Moreover, Divine wisdom and favor are manifested there in a more wonderful and more wondrous manner than they are above ground. Consider how soft the hardest and most unfeeling huge rocks are toward God's commands in the creation and operation of the universe, and how unresisting and flexible they are to the pleasant waters, delicate roots, and silk-like veins that act according to His command. Like a lover, the rock smashes its heart at the touch of those delicate, beautiful things and becomes soft soil in their path.

Also, through the sentence in the verse *and there are some which fall down for awe of God,* the Qur'an displays the tip of a tremendous truth: When Moses asked for a vision of God while standing at the foot of a mountain, the mountain crumbled at the Divine manifestation and its rocks were scattered. Like this, through Divine Majesty's awesome manifestations as earthquakes and similar geological events, rocks fall from summits, which are usually like huge monoliths formed of thickened fluid, and are shattered. Some of these crumble and become fertile soil; others remain as rocks and are scattered down to the valleys and plains.

They serve many purposes for Earth's inhabitants, as in their houses. In utter submission to Divine Power and Wisdom, and for certain hidden purposes and benefits, they stand ready to be used in accordance with the principles of Divine Wisdom. Not in vain, or because of accident or random chance, do they leave their positions at the summit and choose the lower places in humility and become the means of those significant benefits. Rather, they do so out of awe of God.

This shows that such events occur by an All-Wise and All-Powerful One's wise operation, and that there is a wise order invisible to the superficial eye in such seemingly chaotic events. Such are the purposes and benefits attached to these rocks, and the perfect order and fine artistry in the "garments" adorned and embossed with the jewels of fruits and flowers with which the "body" of the mountains down which they roll are clothed.

Thus, you have seen the value of the verse's three parts from the viewpoint of wisdom. See the Qur'an's fine manner of expression and miraculous eloquence, how it shows through the tips of the comprehensive and significant truths mentioned above those three well-known and observed events. Also, by reminding in the same three parts of three further events, each of which is a means of taking a lesson, it offers a fine guidance and restrains in a way that cannot be resisted.

For example, the verse's second part says: *and there are some from which, when they are cleft, water issues.* By referring to the rock cleft with "complete eagerness" when Moses struck it with his staff, and the subsequent pouring forth of twelve streams from twelve sources, it means:

> O Children of Israel. Large rocks become tears out of awe or joy, yet you are so unjust as to remain obstinate when confronted with all of Moses' miracles. You do not weep. Are your eyes so dried and your hearts so hard?

In the third part, it says: *and there are some which fall down for awe of God.* By recalling the well-known event of the mountain crumbling and the rocks rolling down out of awe at the manifestation of Divine Majesty, which took place at Mount Sinai when Moses supplicated for a vision of God, it gives the following lesson:

> O People of Moses. You do not fear God, yet mountains crumble in awe of Him. You witness that He held Mount Sinai above you to receive your solemn promise of loyalty to Him, and that the mountain crumbled when Moses prayed for the Divine vision.

> And yet you are so bold that you do not tremble out of fear of God, and you keep your hearts so hard and unfeeling!

In the first part, it says: *for there are rocks from which rivers gush.* By recalling such rivers as the Nile, the Tigris, and the Euphrates, which gush out of mountains, it points out how wonderfully and miraculously rocks are susceptible and subjugated to the Divine commands of creation. To awakened, attentive hearts, this means:

> The mountains cannot be the actual source of such mighty rivers, for even if they were formed completely of water, they could supply such a river for only a few months. Also rain, which penetrates only about a meter underground, cannot be sufficient income for that high expenditure. No ordinary reason, natural cause, or chance can explain these rivers' sources and flow. The All-Majestic Creator makes them flow forth in truly wonderful fashion from an unseen "treasury."

One Tradition[7] refers to this: "Every minute a drop falls from Paradise into each of those three

---

[7] The Arabic word *hadith*, commonly translated into English as Tradition, literally means news, story, communication, or conversation, whether religious or secular, historical or recent. In the Qur'an, this word appears in religious (39:23, 68:44),

rivers. That is why they flow abundantly." Another Tradition states: "The source of these three rivers is in Paradise."[8] As physical causes cannot produce their abundant flow, their sources must be in an unseen world, a hidden treasury of Mercy, so that the balance between incoming and outgoing water is maintained. By drawing attention to this meaning, the Qur'an gives the following instruction:

> O Children of Israel and children of Adam, your hardness of heart and lack of feeling cause you to disobey the commandments of such a One of Majesty. Your heedlessness causes you to close your eyes to the light of knowledge of such an Everlasting Sun. He causes mighty rivers like the Nile to gush from the mouths of ordinary, solid rocks and turn Egypt into a paradise. For the universe's heart and Earth's mind, He produces miracles of His Power and wit-

secular or general (6:68), historical (20:9), and current or conversational (66:3) contexts. The Prophet used it in a similar sense, for example, when he said: "The best *hadith* is the Qur'an" (Bukhari). However, according to the *Muhaddithin* (Traditionists [scholars of Traditions]), the word stands for "what was transmitted on the Prophet's authority, his deeds, sayings, tacit approvals, or descriptions of his physical appearance." Jurists do not include this last item in their definition. (Tr.)

[8] Recorded by Muslim and Ibn Hanbal.

nesses to His Oneness as strong and abundant as
the gushing forth and flow of those mighty rivers,
and makes them flow to the hearts and minds of
jinn and humanity. Further, while it shows the All-
Majestic Creator as the sunlight shows the sun, that
He makes some hard, unfeeling rocks the objects
of the miracles of His Power in such wonderful
fashion,[9] how is it that you are blind to the light of
His knowledge and do not see the truth?

See how eloquently the Qur'an expresses these
truths. Note the guidance of that eloquence. I wonder what hardness of heart and lack of feeling
cannot be melted by its "heat." If you have understood my words, see one guiding gleam of the
Qur'an's miraculousness and thank God.

---

[9] One of the Nile's main branches rises in the Mountains of
the Moon, the Tigris' main branch rises in a cave in Turkey,
and one of the Euphrates's main streams rises at the foothills
of a mountain in Diyadin. It is scientifically established that
mountains are rocks solidified from liquid matter. One of the
Prophet's glorifications—Glory be to the One Who spread
out soil on solidified liquid—testifies that Earth's original
formation is as follows: Some liquid matter solidified at
Divine command and became rock, and then rock became soil.
In other words, the liquid matter was too soft to settle on, and
the rock was too hard to benefit from. Therefore, the All-Wise
and Compassionate One spread soil over the rock and made
it a place of habitation for living beings.

Glory be to You. We have no knowledge save what You have taught us. Truly, you are the All-Knowing, the All-Wise. O God, enable us to understand the mysteries of the Qur'an as You like and approve, and grant us success in the service of it. Amen, through Your Mercy, O Merciful of the Merciful. O God, bestow blessings and peace upon the one to whom the wise Qur'an was sent, and upon his Family and Companions.

**SECOND STATION:** (A gleam of the Qur'an's miraculousness, which shines through the Prophets' miracles.) Notice the two questions and their answers at the end.

\*\*\*

In the name of God,
the Merciful, the Compassionate.

Not a thing, fresh or withered, wet or dry, but it is in a Manifest Book. (6:59)

Several years ago in my *Isharat al-I'jaz* (Signs of Miraculousness), I discussed in Arabic one meaning of this verse.[10] Now two of my brothers-in-religion, whose wishes are important to me, have asked for a Turkish explanation of that discussion. Relying

_____

[10] *Isharat al-I'jaz*: Commentary on *Surat al-Fatiha* and the initial 30 verses of *Surat al-Baqara*.

on Almighty God's help, and based on the Qur'an's enlightenment, I write the following section.

According to one interpretation, the Manifest Book is the Qur'an. This verse states that everything is found in it. This is true. However, we must realize that things are found at different levels. They are presented as seeds, nuclei, summaries, principles or signs, as well as explicitly or implicitly, allusively, vaguely or suggestively. Depending on the occasion, one form is preferred to best convey the Qur'an's purposes and meet the context's requirements.

For example, progress in science and industry has resulted in airplanes, electricity, motorized transportation, and radio and telecommunication. Such things are prominent in our daily lives. As the Qur'an addresses humanity [at all times], it does not ignore these developments; rather, it points to them through the Prophets' miracles and in connection with certain historical events.

> Down with the makers of the trench of the fuel-fed fire. When they sat by it, and were themselves the witnesses of what they did to the believers. They ill-treated them for no other reason than that they

> believed in God, the Mighty, the All-Praised One. (85:4-8)[11]

> ... in the loaded fleet. And We have created for them the like thereof, whereon they ride. (36:41-42)

Such verses point to trains, while the following verse, besides its many other meanings and connotations, alludes to electricity:

> God is the Light of the heavens and Earth. The parable of His Light is as a niche wherein is a lamp. The lamp is in a glass, and the glass is, as it were, a shining star kindled from a blessed olive tree, neither of the East or the West, whose oil would almost glow forth (of itself) though no fire touched it: Light upon light.[12] God guides to His Light whom He wills. (24:35)

Since many people have analyzed verses of the second type, those alluding to modern technology in connection with historical events, and since they require much care and detailed explanation,

---

[11] These verses allude to trains, which offered great advantage to the unbelievers in bringing the Muslim world under their control.

[12] The phrases: *whose oil would almost glow forth (of itself) though no fire touched it: Light upon light* makes the allusion clearer.

as well as being very numerous, I shall content myself with verses alluding to trains and electricity as seen in the Qur'anic accounts of the Prophets' miracles.

## Introduction

God Almighty sent the Prophets as leaders and vanguards of spiritual and moral progress, and thus endowed them with certain wonders and miracles and made them masters and forerunners of humanity's material progress. He commands people to follow them absolutely.

By relating the Prophets' spiritual and moral perfections, the Qur'an encourages people to benefit from them. By presenting their miracles, it urges people to achieve something similar through science. It may even be said that, like spiritual and moral attainments, material attainments and wonders were first given to humanity as gifts through Prophetic miracles. For example, Noah was the first to build ships, and Joseph was the first to build clocks. Thus the ship and clock were given first as Prophetic miracles. It is a meaningful indication of this reality that so many craft guilds take a Prophet as the "patron" or originator of their craft. For example, seamen take Noah, watchmakers take Joseph, and tailors take Enoch.

Since truth-seeking scholars and the science of eloquence agree that each Qur'anic verse contains guidance and instruction, it follows that verses relating the Prophets' miracles, the most brilliant of all verses, should not be considered mere historical events. Rather, they comprise numerous indications of guidance. By relating these miracles, the Qur'an shows the ultimate goal of scientific and technological developments, and specifies their final aims, toward which it urges humanity. Just as the past is the field for the future's seeds and the mirror to its potential picture, so is the future the time to reap the past life's harvest and the mirror to the actual situation. Out of many examples, I shall point out only a few.

The verse: *And to Solomon (We subjugated) the wind: its morning stride was a month's journey and the evening stride was a month's journey* (34:12) expresses the wind's subjugation to Solomon: Solomon covered the distance of 2 months' walk in two strides by flying through the air. This suggests that humanity can and should strive to travel through the air. Almighty God also is saying: "One of My servants did not obey his carnal desires, and I mounted him on the air. If you give up laziness and benefit properly from certain of My laws in nature, you too can mount it."

The verse: *When Moses asked for water for his people, We said: "Strike the rock with your staff." Then gushed forth therefrom twelve springs (so that) each tribe knew their drinking place"* (2:60) indicates that simple tools can unlock Mercy's underground treasuries. In places hard as rock, the water for life may be drawn with so simple a device as a staff. Through this meaning, the verse urges us to seek these treasures. Through this verse, God Almighty suggests: "One of My servants relied on Me, and so I gave him a staff that draws the water for life from wherever he wishes. If you rely on My laws of Mercy, you too can obtain such a device." Modern scientists have invented many devices to bring up subsurface water. The verse points to further goals, just as the previous one specified attainments far ahead of today's airplanes.

The verse: *I heal him who was born blind, and the leper, and I raise the dead by God's leave* (3:49), concerning a miracle of Jesus, alludes to and encourages the highest level of healing with which God endowed him. It suggests that even the most chronic ailments can be cured. Therefore, we should search for it. By the verse God Almighty means:

> I gave two gifts to one of My servants who renounced the world for My sake: the remedy for spiritual ailments, and the cure for physical sicknesses. Dead hearts were quickened through the light of guidance, and sick people who were as though dead found health through his breath and cure. You may find the cure for all illnesses in My "pharmacy" in nature, where I attached many important purposes to each thing. Work and find it.

This verse marks the final point of medical development far ahead of the present level and urges us toward it.

The verses: *We made iron supple for him [David]* (34:10), *We gave him [David] wisdom and sound judgment in speech and decision* (38:20), and *We caused the fount of copper to gush forth with him [Solomon]* (34:12) indicate that softening iron is one of God's greatest bounties, one through which He shows a great Prophet's virtue. Softening iron, smelting copper, and extracting minerals is the origin, source, and basis of all material industries. These verses state that these two processes are great favors granted to two great Prophets, who ruled according to God's commandments, and are the means to most general industries.

Since God endowed a Prophet, who was both a spiritual and political leader, with wise speech, craftsmanship, and industry, He urges people to speak wisely and encourages them toward craftsmanship and industry. By these verses, God Almighty suggests:

> I gave such wisdom to the tongue and heart of a servant who obeyed My religious commandments to judge and distinguish between all things with perfect clarity and to discern the truth. I endowed him with such skill that he could cast iron into any mold and then use it as an important source of strength for his rule.

> Since this is possible and since iron has great significance for your social life, which requires it, such wisdom and skill will be bestowed on you if you obey My commands of creation, My laws of nature. Eventually you will attain it.

By softening iron and smelting copper, humanity has achieved great industrial progress and material power. These verses direct our attention toward this truth. Just as they warned earlier peoples who did not appreciate its importance, so they warn today's lazy people.

The verse: *One with whom was knowledge of the Book said: "I will bring it to you before your gaze returns to you (in the twinkling of an eye)." When Solomon saw it set in his presence...* (27:40), describes the wonderful event of bringing the Queen of Sheba's throne to Solomon's court. This suggests that things can be transported over long distances, either bodily or in their images. In fact, God Almighty bestowed this as a miracle upon Solomon, who was honored with kingship as well as Divine Messengership, so that he could maintain his infallibility and justice by being personally informed of all regions in his extensive realm, see his subjects' conditions, and hear of their troubles.

That means that if we rely on Almighty God and appeal to Him in the tongue of our potentials, as Solomon did in the tongue of his infallibility, and if our acts conform to His laws in the universe and with what attracts His favor, the world may become like a town for us. The Queen's throne was in Yemen, yet it was seen in Damascus either bodily or in image, as were the forms of the people around it, who were seen and heard.

This verse points to the transport of forms and transmission of sounds over long distances. In effect, it says: "O rulers. If you wish to realize perfect justice, try to see and know your realm in all its details, as Solomon did. Only by rising to such a level can a just ruler who cherishes his subjects be saved from being held accountable. Only in this manner may he realize perfect justice." God Almighty means:

> O humanity. I bestowed on My servant a vast realm. So that he might realize perfect justice throughout it, I allowed him to know whatever was happening therein. Since I have created every person with a capacity to rule according to My commands, I also have given him, as a requirement of My Wisdom, the potential to scan Earth's face and comprehend whatever is in it. If every person cannot reach this point, humanity as a species may realize it. If they do not achieve it physically, they can do it spiritually, like the saints. Therefore, you may benefit from this great blessing. Come on, let Me see you do it. Fulfill your duties of worship. Strive in such a way that you may turn Earth's face into a garden, every part of which you may see, and the sounds from every corner of which you may hear. Heed the decree of the Most Merciful: He made Earth subservient to you, so walk in the paths thereof and eat of His providence. Unto Him is the resurrection. (67:15)

Thus the verse mentioned above marks the ultimate point in the transmission of images and sounds, which constitutes one of the latest and most significant developments in science and technology, and encourages humanity toward that furthest point.

The verses: *Others linked together in chains* (38:38) and: *Of the evil ones were some who dived for him, and did other work* (21:82), state that Solomon made the jinn, devils, and evil spirits obey him. He prevented their evil and used them for beneficial work. In other words: The jinn, who are conscious beings and Earth's most important inhabitants after humanity, may serve us and can be contacted. Devils also may be made to serve, either willingly or unwillingly. God Almighty made them obey a servant who obeyed His commands. These verses imply: "O humanity. I made jinn and devils, including their most evil ones, obey a servant who obeyed Me. If you submit yourself to My commands, most creatures, including jinn and devils, may be subjugated to you."

These verses mark the highest point in the occult or supernatural sciences dealing with paranormal events, which appear as a blend of art and science and out of our extraordinary material and spiritual sensitivity. They urge us to subjugate and employ such beings through the Qur'an so that we may be saved from their evil.

These verses, and others like: *Then We sent to her Our spirit and it assumed for her the form of a perfect man* (19:17), hint that spirit beings may assume visible forms. But the Qur'an is not alluding to modern necromancy, which some "civilized" people practice by trying to contact the spirits of the dead, for these, in reality, are evil spirits masquerading as the dead person. Rather, it is the form known to certain saints, like Muhiy al-Din ibn al-'Arabi, who could communicate with good spirits at will, make contact and form relations with them, and, by going to their abodes and drawing near to their atmosphere, benefit from their spirituality.

The verses: *We subdued the hills to hymn the praises (of their Lord) with him at nightfall and after sunrise* (38:18), *O you mountains. Echo His psalms of praise, and you birds. And We made the iron supple for him* (34:10), and *We have been taught the language of birds* (27:16), which are about David's miracles, point out that Almighty God gave David's glorifications such strength and such a resonant and pleasing tone that they brought the mountains to ecstasy. Like a huge sound system, each mountain formed a circle around the chief reciter—David—and repeated his glorifications. This is a reality, for every mountain with caves can "speak" like a parrot. If you declare before a mountain: "All praise be to God," the mountain will echo it back. Since God Almighty has granted this ability to mountains, it can be developed.

God endowed David with both Messengership and caliphate in an exceptional form. Thus He made this seed of ability flourish as a miracle with that comprehensive Messengership and magnificent sovereignty that great mountains followed him like soldiers, students, or disciples. Under his direction and in his tongue, they glorified the All-Majestic Creator and repeated whatever he said.

At present, due to advancements in communication, a great commander can get a large army dispersed through the mountains to repeat his declaration "God is the Greatest" at the same time, and make the mountains speak and ring with the words. If an ordinary commander can do this, a magnificent commander of Almighty God can get them actually to utter and recite God's glorifications. Besides, each mountain has a collective personality and corporate identity, and offers glorifications and worship unique to itself. Just as each one glorifies in humanity's tongue via echoing, it also glorifies the All-Majestic Creator in its own particular tongue.

The verses: *We have been taught the tongues of birds* (27:16) and *The birds assembled* (38:19) point out that Almighty God bestowed on David and Solomon knowledge of the birds' languages and of the tongues of abilities (how they could be of benefit). Given this, and that Earth is a laden table of the Most Merciful One set up in our honor, most animals and birds that benefit from this table may serve us. God uses such small animals as honeybees and silkworms, through the guidance of His special inspiration, to benefit humanity. By enabling us to use pigeons and make certain birds like parrots speak, He has added to the beauty of human civilization.

If we could discover how to use other birds and animals, many species might be employed for important tasks, just as domestic animals are. For example, if the languages of locust-destroying starlings were known and their movements could be controlled, they could be used against plagues of locusts. What a valuable free service this would be! Thus, the verses mentioned show the ultimate point in subjugating and benefiting from birds, and making such lifeless beings speak like a telephone. By specifying the farthest aim in this field, the verses urge humanity toward it.

By the same verses, God Almighty indicates:

> So that his infallibility as a Prophet and his justice as a sovereign might not be damaged, I subjugated to one of your fellow men, who was totally submitted to Me, the huge creatures in My Kingdom and made them speak. I put most of My troops and animals in his service. I have entrusted to each of you the Supreme Trust[13] that the heavens, Earth, and the mountains refused, and have endowed you with the potential to rule on Earth according to My commands. Therefore you should yield to the One in Whose hand are the reins of all creatures. This will cause the creatures in His Kingdom to yield to you, so that you may use them in the name of the One Who holds their reins and rise to a position worthy of your potential.

---

[13] The Supreme Trust is our ego or human identity, which includes free will, knowledge, intellect, and speech. For an elaboration on this topic, consult The Thirtieth Word. (Tr.)

Given this, do not waste your time with record players, musical instruments, playing with pigeons, making parrots speak, and so on. Rather, try for a most agreeable, elevated, and sacred amusement—that mountains may function as a huge sound system for you as they did for David, that a breeze may cause the tunes of Divine praise and glorification to reach your ears from trees and plants, that mountains may manifest themselves as wonderful creatures reciting Divine glorifications in thousands of tongues, and that most birds may be each an intimate friend or an obedient servant, like Solomon's hoopoe. They may entertain you and drive you with zeal toward the perfections and attainments of which you are capable, rather than causing you to fall from the position required by your humanity, as vain amusements do.

The verse: *We said: "O fire. Be coolness and peace for Abraham"* (21:69), about one of Abraham's miracles, contains three subtle indications:

*FIRST:* Like every element in nature, fire performs a duty under a command. It did not burn Abraham, for God commanded it not to do so.

*SECOND:* One type of heat burns through coldness. Through the phrase Be peace, God Almighty ordered the cold: "Like heat, do not burn him."[14]

---

[14] An interpreter of the Qur'an remarks: "If He had not said: *Be peace,* it would have burned him with its coldness."

It is simultaneously fire and cold. Science has discovered a fire called "white heat," which does not radiate its heat. Instead, by attracting the surrounding heat, it causes the surrounding area to become cold enough to freeze liquids and in effect burns them through its cold. (Hell, which contains all degrees and sorts of fire, also must have this intense cold.)

*THIRD:* Just as there is an immaterial substance like belief and an armor like Islam, which will remove and protect against the effects of Hellfire, there must be a physical substance that will protect against and prevent the effects of fire. As is required by His Name the All-Wise, and since this world is the Abode of Wisdom, [where everything occurs for a definite purpose and usually according to cause and effect], God Almighty acts behind the veil of cause and effect. Therefore, as the fire did not burn Abraham's body or clothes, He gave them a state that resisted fire.

Thus the verse suggests:

> O nation of Abraham. Be like Abraham, so that your garments may be your guard against the fire, your greatest enemy, in both worlds. Coat your spirit with belief, and it will be your armor against Hell-fire.

> Moreover, Earth contains substances that will pro-
> tect you from fire's evil. Search for them, extract
> them, and coat yourselves with them.

As an important step in his progress, humanity discovered a fire-resistant substance. But see
how elevated, fine, and beautiful a garment this
verse points to, which will be woven on the loom
of purity of belief in and submission to God, and
which will not be rent for all eternity.

The verse: *He taught Adam all the names* (2:31)
states that, as his greatest miracle in the cause of
supreme vicegerency, Adam was taught the names.
While other Prophets' miracles point to a particular wonder in the course of scientific and technological progress, the miracle of Adam, the father
of all Prophets and the Opening of the Office of
Prophethood, alludes almost explicitly to the ultimate points and final goals of human attainment
and progress. By this verse, God Almighty suggests:

> O children of Adam. To prove his superiority over
> the angels as regards vicegerency, I taught Adam
> all the Names.[15] Being his children and inheritors

---

[15] The Names taught to Adam are the names of things as the
keys to human knowledge. They originate in Divine Names,
each one the source of a branch of science. For example,

of his abilities, learn all the names and show that you are worthy of this superiority over all other creatures, such that vast creatures like Earth are made obedient to you. Step forward, hold on to one of My Names, and rise. Adam was deceived by Satan once and for all, and temporarily fell to Earth from an abode like the Garden. So do not follow Satan in your progress, thereby making it the means of falling from the heavens of Divine Wisdom into the misguidance of attributing creativity to nature, or real effect to cause and effect in the creation and operation of nature. Raise your head and, studying My Beautiful Names, make science and your progress steps by which to ascend to the heavens. Then you may rise to My Names of Lordship, which are the essences and sources of your science and attainments, and through them look to your Lord with your hearts.

## A significant point and important mystery

In describing all the attainments of learning, scientific progress, and wonders of technology with which we have been endowed because of our vast potential under the title of "the teaching of the Names," the above verse alludes to a fine point:

---

medicine has its source in the Name the All-Healing, and engineering in the Names the All-Determiner and the Giver of Certain Measure. (Tr.)

Each attainment, perfection, learning, progress, and science has an elevated reality based on a Divine Name. Manifesting itself through veils and in various ways and levels, a particular branch of science or art attains its perfection and becomes reality. Otherwise it remains imperfect, deficient, and shadowy.

For example, engineering's reality lies in the Divine Names the All-Just (One Who gives everything a certain measure and creates everything in its place) and the Determiner. Its final aim is to receive the wise manifestations of those Names in full measure and with all their majesty. Medicine is an art and a science. Its reality lies in the Divine Name the All-Healing, and its perfection in finding a cure for every illness by discovering the manifestations of the Absolutely Wise One's mercy in Earth, His vast "pharmacy."

Each natural science, which discusses the reality of entities, can be a true science full of wisdom only by discerning the regulating, directing, administering, sustaining, and all-embracing manifestations of the Divine Name the All-Wise in things; in the benefits and advantages of those things; and by being based on that Name. Otherwise they

become superstition and nonsense, or, like natu-
ralistic philosophy, cause misguidance. Compare
these three examples with other sciences and attainments.

With this verse, the wise Qur'an points to the
highest points, the furthest limits, the final degrees—
from which we are still far removed—and urges
us toward them. This verse is extremely rich and
elaborate in meaning, but for now I will go no
further.

The Qur'an is the Prophet's[16] supreme miracle,
the seal of the Office of Prophethood, the leader
of Prophets, and the cause of pride of all beings.
When compared with his cause of Messengership,
all Prophets' miracles are like one miracle. He was
endowed in full with all levels of all Names taught,
in brief, to Adam. By raising his finger in a mood

---

[16] In any publication dealing with Prophet Muhammad, his
name or title is followed by "upon him be peace and blessings," to show our respect for him and because it is a religious requirement. For his Companions and other illustrious Muslims: "May God be pleased with him (or her)" is
used. However, as this might be distracting to non-Muslim
readers, these phrases do not appear in this book, on the
understanding that they are assumed and that no disrespect
is intended. (Ed.)

of majesty, the Prophet split the moon; by lowering it in a display of grace, he made water flow from it abundantly; and he was verified and corroborated by hundreds of miracles. Many verses like: *Say: "If people and jinn banded together to produce the like of this Qur'an, they would never produce its like, not though they backed each other"* (17:88) express its pure explanation, eloquent expression, comprehensive meanings, and sublime and sweet styles. Together, these constitute one of the Qur'an's most brilliant aspects.

Such verses attract people and jinn to the most manifest and brilliant aspects of that Eternal Miracle. It provokes them, stirring up the zeal of its friends and the obstinacy of its enemies. It encourages and stimulates them to produce something resembling it. It places that miracle before the eyes of creatures, as if humanity's only aim is to take it as our goal and guiding principle in life, to study so that we can advance consciously and knowingly to the goal destined in creation.

Briefly, the other Prophets' miracles point to a wonder of human arts or crafts and technology. Adam's miracle indicates a concise, summarized form of those crafts' basis, as well as the indexes

of sciences, branches of knowledge, and wonders and perfections, and urges us toward them.

The Qur'an of Miraculous Expression, the
supreme miracle of Muhammad, the object of all
the Divine Names' manifestations in their fullness, shows fully the true goal of science and all
branches of knowledge, as well as the perfections,
attainments, and happiness of both worlds. It urges
us toward them in such a way that it means:

> O people, the sublime aim in creating this universe
> is your response to Divine Lordship's manifestation
> (administering, directing, training, and sustaining)
> with universal worship. Your ultimate aim is to real-
> ize that worship through science, attainment, and
> perfections.

The Qur'an also hints at this: "At the end of time,
humanity will pour into science and learning.
People will derive all strength from science. Power
and rule will pass to the hand of science and knowledge." By frequently emphasizing its eloquent
and beautiful style, the Qur'an suggests: "At the
end of time, eloquence and beauty of expression, the
most brilliant sciences and branches of knowledge,
will be most sought after in all their varieties. People
will find that when it comes to making each other

accept their opinions and exercise their rule, their most effective weapon will be eloquent expression; their most irresistible force will be fine oratory."

In short, most Qur'anic verses are keys to a treasury of perfections and a store of knowledge. If you want to ascend to the Qur'an's sky and reach the stars of its verses, make these 20 Words a 20-step stairway and climb them. You will see what a brilliant, shining sun the Qur'an is. Notice how it radiates a pure light over the Divine truths and the truths of the contingent (created) realm. See what a brilliant light it spreads.

Thus, since the verses concerning the Prophets allude to contemporary technology's wonders and have a manner of expression that suggests their furthest limits, since each verse has many meanings, and since there are categorical commands to follow and obey the Prophets, the verses mentioned above must be pointing to the importance of human arts and sciences, in addition to their literal meanings, and urging us toward them.

**Two important answers to two important questions**

QUESTION: Since the Qur'an was sent for humanity, why does it not mention explicitly the wonders of civilization that we consider important? Why does it content itself with allusions, indications, or references?

**ANSWER:** The Qur'an does so because it discusses each topic according to its worth in its eyes. Its basic duty is to teach Divine Lordship's perfections, Essential Qualities, and acts, as well as servanthood's duties, status, and affairs. Thus the wonders of human civilization merit only a slight indication or implicit reference or allusion.

For example, if an airplane appealed to the Qur'an: "Give me the right to speak and a place in your verses," the aircraft of Lordship's sphere (e.g., planets, Earth, the moon) would reply on the Qur'an's behalf: "You may have a place in proportion to your size."[17] If a submarine asked for a place, submarines belonging to that sphere (e.g., heavenly bodies "swimming" in the vast "ocean" of the atmosphere and ether) would say: "Your place beside us is too small to be visible." If a shining, star-like electric light asked to be included, the

_____

[17] While discussing this serious subject, my pen involuntarily slipped into this light manner of writing, and I let it go. I hope this does not detract from the subject's seriousness.

electric lights of that sphere (e.g., lightning, shoot-ing stars, and stars adorning the sky) would say: "You have a right to be mentioned and spoken of only in proportion to your light."

If the wonders of human civilization demand-ed a place with respect to the fineness of their art, a fly would reply: "Be quiet, for even one of my wings has more of a right than you do. If all of your fine arts and delicate instruments were joined together, they could not be as wonderful and as exquisite as the fine art and delicate members con-centrated in my tiny body." The verse: *Surely those upon whom you call, apart from God, shall nev-er create (even) a fly, though they banded togeth-er to do it* (22:73) will silence you."

If those wonders appealed to the Sphere of Servanthood, they would receive a reply like the following:

> You have very little relationship with us, so you cannot enter our sphere. Our program is this: The world is a guest-house. Humanity is a guest with many duties. Each person will stay there for a short time. Being charged with preparing themselves for eternal life, they will give priority to their most urgent and important duties. As you mostly seem to be designed in heedlessness and world-mindedness,

as if the world were eternal, you have very little share in servanthood to and worship of God, which is founded upon love of truth and otherworldliness.

However, if there are among you respected crafts-people, scientists, and inspired inventors, who, pure-ly for the benefit of God's servants, serve the gen-eral interest and public ease and attainment of social life, which is a valuable sort of worship, the Qur'an's allusions and indications are sufficient for such sensitive people, who are a minority among their colleagues, to encourage them and honor their accom-plishments.

**QUESTION:** You might ask: "After these dis-cussions, I understand that the Qur'an contains, along with all other truths and indications of, as well as allusions to, modern civilization's most advanced wonders. Everything necessary for human happi-ness in both worlds is found in it, in proportion to its worth. But why does the Qur'an not mention them explicitly, so that everyone would believe and our minds would be eased?"

**ANSWER:** Religion is for examination, a test and trial offered by God to distinguish elevated and base spirits from each other. Just as raw materi-als are fired to separate diamonds from coal and gold from soil, Divine obligations test conscious beings so that the precious "ore" in the "mine" of human potential may be separated from the dross. Since the Qur'an was sent for humanity to be perfected through trial, it only alludes to future events pertaining to the world, which everyone will witness. It only opens the door to reason as much as needed to prove its argument.

If it had mentioned such things explicitly, testing would be meaningless. They would be so clear, as if writing *There is no deity but God* on the face of the sky with stars, that everyone would be forced to believe. There would be no competition, and the testing and trial would mean nothing. A coal-like spirit would stay with and appear to be equal to a diamond-like spirit.[18]

In short, the Qur'an is wise and gives everything a position in proportion to its value. Thus, 1,300 years ago it saw the extent of human progress and its fruits, which were hidden in the darkness of the Unseen (the future), and showed them in a better form. This shows that the Qur'an is the Word of

---

[18] Abu Jahl the Accursed and Abu Bakr the Truthful would appear to be equal, and the purpose for testing people and accounting them responsible for their free acts would become meaningless.

One Who sees at the same instant all time and all within it.

All that we have explained so far is only one gleam of the Qur'an's miraculousness, which shines on the "face" of the Prophets' miracles.

> O God. Enable us to understand the Qur'an's mysteries and make us successful in serving it at every instant and at all times. Glory be to You. We have no knowledge save what You have taught us. Truly, you are the All-Knowing, the All-Wise.
>
> O God. Bestow blessings, peace, benedictions, and honor on our master and lord, Muhammad, Your servant and Prophet and Messenger, the unlettered Prophet, on his Family and Companions and wives and descendants; on all other Prophets and Messengers; on the angels made near unto You; and on the saints and the righteous.
>
> Bestow on them the most excellent of blessings, the purest peace, and the most abundant benedictions, to the number of the Qur'an's suras, verses, words, letters, meanings, indications, allusions, and references. Forgive us, have mercy on us, and be gracious to us, our God, our Creator, for the sake of each of those blessings, through Your Mercy, O Most Merciful of the Merciful. All praise be to God, the Lord of the Worlds. Amen.

# The Miraculous Qur'an

> While we have an eternal miracle like the Qur'an,
> I feel no need for any other proof.
> While we have an evidence of truth like the Qur'an,
> I feel no difficulty in silencing those who deny.

NOTE: The verses discussed in this treatise are those that have been criticized or questioned. Their truths are herein explained in such a way that these very points are shown to be, in reality, the rays of miraculousness and the sources of the Qur'an's eloquence.

Doubts based on such pretexts as the sun runs ... and the mountains as masts, through which they seek to cast doubt on the Qur'an's authenticity and authorship, are removed.

Since this treatise was composed quickly and amid troubled circumstances, there may be some defects in the expression of ideas. However, it explains several issues that have great scientific importance, and so may be of use even in its present form.

— Said Nursi

In the name of God,
the Merciful, the Compassionate.

Say: "If humanity and jinn banded together to produce the like of this Qur'an, they would never produce its like, even though they backed one another." (17:88)

Out of countless aspects of the Qur'an's miraculousness, which is a store of miracles and the greatest miracle of Prophet Muhammad, I have so far mentioned about 40 in my Arabic treatises, *Isharat al-I'jaz* (Signs of Miraculousness, an introductory commentary on the Qur'an) and in the previous 24 Words. I will explain only five here, which briefly mention the others, following an introductory definition of the Qur'an.

## Three parts

### First part

**QUESTION:** Will you please define the Qur'an?

**ANSWER:** As explained in The Nineteenth Word and argued elsewhere, the Qur'an is an eternal translation of the great Book of the Universe[19] and the everlasting translator of the "languages" in which the Divine laws of the universe's creation and operation are "inscribed"; the interpreter of the books of the visible, material world and the World of the Unseen; the discloser of the imma-terial treasuries of the Divine Names hidden on Earth and in the heavens; the key to the truths lying beneath the lines of events; the World of the Unseen's tongue in the visible, material one; the treasury of the All-Merciful One's favors and the All-Glorified One's eternal addresses coming from the World of the Unseen beyond the veil of

---

[19] In Said Nursi's thought, God created the universe as a "book" to be "read" by those who want to learn of and draw close to Him. The universe's order, regularity, interconnect-edness, functioning, and so on display some of his Names and Attributes. Others are displayed through the animate and inan-imate members of His creation, such as the All-Compassionate, All-Providing, All-Merciful, Forgiver, and so on. (Ed.)

this visible world; the sun of Islam's spiritual and intellectual worlds, as well as its foundation and plan; the sacred map of the Hereafter's worlds; the expounder, lucid interpreter, articulate proof, and clear translator of the Divine Essence, Attributes, Names and acts; the educator and trainer of humanity's world and the water and light of Islam, the true and greatest humanity; and the true wisdom of humanity and the true guide leading them to happiness.

For humanity, it is a book of law, prayer, wisdom, worship and servanthood to God, commands and invitation, invocation and reflection. It is a holy book containing books for all of our spiritual needs; a heavenly book that, like a sacred library, contains numerous booklets from which all saints, eminently truthful people, all purified and discerning scholars, and those well-versed in knowledge of God have derived their own specific ways, and which illuminate each way and answer their followers' needs.

### Second part

Having come from God's Supreme Throne, originated in His Greatest Name, and issued from each

Name's most comprehensive rank, and as explained in The Twelfth Word, the Qur'an is God's word (as regards His being the Lord of the worlds) and His decree (in respect of His having the title of Deity of all creatures). It is a discourse in the name of the Creator of the heavens and Earth, a speech from the view of absolute Divine Lordship, and an eternal sermon on behalf of the All-Glorified One's universal Sovereignty. It is also a register of the Most Merciful One's favors from the viewpoint of all-embracing Mercy; a collection of messages, some of which begin with a cipher; and a holy book that, having descended from the Divine Greatest Name's surrounding circle, looks over and surveys the circle surrounded by His Supreme Throne.

This is why the title "the Word of God" has been (and will always be) given to the Qur'an. After the Qur'an come the Scriptures and Pages sent to other Prophets. Some of the other countless Divine words are inspirations coming as particular displays of a particular aspect of Divine Mercy, Sovereignty, and Lordship under a particular title and with a particular regard. The inspirations coming to angels, people, and animals vary greatly with regard to their universality or particularity.

### Third part

The Qur'an briefly contains all Scriptures revealed to previous Prophets, the content of all saints' treatises, and all purified scholars' works. Its six sides are bright and absolutely free of doubt and whimsical thought. Its point of support is Divine Revelation and the Divine eternal Word, whose aim is eternal happiness and whose inside is pure guidance. It is surrounded and supported from above by the lights of belief, from below by proof and evidence, from the right by the heart's submission and the conscience, and from the left by the admission of reason and other intellectual faculties.

Its fruit is the Most Merciful One's Mercy and Paradise. It has been accepted and promoted by angels and innumerable people and jinn throughout the centuries.

All of these qualities mentioned above have been proven in other places or will be proved in the following pages.

### First light

This Light has three rays.

### First ray

This is the Qur'an's miraculous eloquence, which originates in its words' beauty, order, and composition; its textual beauty and perfection; its stylistic originality and uniqueness; its explanations' superiority, excellence, and clarity; its meanings' power and truth; and its linguistic purity and fluency. Its eloquence is so extraordinary that its eternal challenge to every individual to produce something like it, even if only a chapter, has yet to be answered. Instead, those geniuses who, in their self-pride and self-confidence, consider themselves equal to the task eventually have had to humble themselves before it.

I point out its miraculous eloquence in two ways:

**FIRST WAY:** The people of Arabia were mostly unlettered at that time, and so preserved their tribal pride, history, and proverbs in oral poetry. They attached great importance to eloquence, and so any meaningful, unique expression was memorized for its poetical form and eloquence and then handed down to posterity. Eloquence and fluency were in such great demand that a tribe treated its eloquent literary figures as national heroes.

Those intelligent people, who would govern a considerable portion of the world after Islam's advent, were more eloquent than other nations. Eloquence was so esteemed that two tribes would sometimes go to war over a saying of a literary figure and then be reconciled by the words of another. They even inscribed in gold the odes of seven poets and hung them on the wall of the Ka'ba.[20]

At a time when eloquence was in such demand, the Qur'an of miraculous explanation was revealed. Just as God Almighty had endowed Moses and Jesus with the miracles most suitable to their times, He made eloquence the most notable aspect of the Qur'an, the chief miracle of Prophet Muhammad.[21] When it was revealed, it challenged first the literary figures of the Arabian peninsula: *If you doubt what We have sent down on Our servant, produce a sura like it* (2:23). It defeated their intellectual pretensions and humbled them by continuing: *If you cannot, and you certainly cannot, fear the Fire,*

---

[20] These seven odes were called the Seven Suspended Poems.

[21] Moses was given the miracles of the staff and white hand, because in his time sorcery was in great demand. Jesus was given the miracles of raising the dead and healing certain illnesses, for in his time healing was highly favored.

*whose fuel is people and stones, prepared for unbe-
lievers* (2:24).

Those self-conceited people could not argue
verbally with the Qur'an. Although this was an easy
and safe course to obstruct and falsify its message,
they chose to fight it with swords, the perilous and
most difficult course. If those intelligent people,
skilled in diplomacy, could have argued verbally
with the Qur'an, they would not have chosen the
perilous, difficult course and risked losing their
property and lives. Since they could not, they had
to choose the more dangerous way.

There were two powerful reasons for trying to
produce something like the Qur'an: to refute its
claim of Revelation (its enemies) and to imitate
it (its friends). The result was, and continues to be,
innumerable books written in Arabic. All people,
whether scholars or not, who read such books are
forced to admit that they do not resemble the
Qur'an. So, either the Qur'an is inferior—friend and
foe admit that this is inconceivable—or superior
to all of them. There are no other options.

*QUESTION:* How do we know that people have
never dared to dispute with it, and that their coop-
erative effort failed?

*Answer:* If this were possible, disputants would have appeared. Since so many people have opposed the truth, such an attempt would have found many supporters and been well known. When even an insignificant struggle arouses great curiosity, such a historic, unusual contest could not have been kept secret. Although the most insignificant and detestable objections concerning Islam have been circulated widely, nothing other than a few pieces of Musaylima the Liar have been narrated.[22] Whatever his oratorical skills, the historical record of his words show them as utter absurdities when compared with the Qur'an's infinitely beautiful expressions. Thus the Qur'an's miraculous eloquence is indisputable.

**Second way:** Now we explain in five points the wisdom in the Qur'an's miraculous eloquence.

*First point:* There is an extraordinary eloquence and stylistic purity in the Qur'an's word order or composition. This is explained in my *Isharat al-I'jaz.* Just as a clock's hands complete and are fit-

---

[22] Musaylima the Liar claimed that he had been made a partner with the Prophet in authority and composed some "suras." The Prophet rejected him, and Musaylima was killed during the battle of al-Yamama (633), which occurred during Abu Bakr's caliphate. (Tr.)

ted to each other in precise orderliness, so does every word and sentence—indeed the whole Qur'an—complete and fit each other.

This extraordinary eloquence is visible for all to see. Consider the following examples:

• From *Surat al-Anbiya'*:

> If but a breath from the punishment of Your Lord touches them. (21:46)

To indicate the severity of God's punishment, the above clause points to the least amount or slightest element of it. As the entire clause expresses this slightness, all of its parts should reinforce that meaning.

*If but* (*la'in*) signify uncertainty and thus imply slightness (of punishment). *Massa* means to touch slightly, also signifying slightness. *Nafhatun* (a breath) is merely a puff of air. Grammatically derived from the word used to express singleness, it also underlies the slightness. The double *n* (*tanwin*) at the end of *nafhatun* indicates indefiniteness and suggests that it is slight and insignificant. *Min* implies a part or a piece, thus indicating paucity. *'Adhab* (torment or punishment) is light in meaning compared to *nakal* (exemplary chastisement) and *'iqab* (heavy penalty), and denotes a light punishment or torment. Using *Rabb* (Lord, Provider, Sustainer), suggesting affection, instead of (for example) Overwhelming, All-Compelling, or Avenger, also expresses slightness.

Finally, the clause means that if so slight a breath of torment or punishment has such an affect, one should reflect how severe the Divine chastisement might be. We see in this short clause how its parts are related to each other and add to the meaning. This example concerns the words chosen and the purpose in choosing them.

• From *Surat al-Baqara*:

> They give as sustenance out of what We have bestowed on them (as livelihood). (2:3)

The parts of the above sentence point to five conditions that make alms-giving acceptable to God.

**First condition:** While giving alms, believers must not give so much that they are reduced to begging. *Out of* expresses this.

**Second condition:** They must give out of what they have, not out of what others have. *We have bestowed on them* points to this. The meaning is give (to sustain life) out of what We have given you (to sustain your life).

**Third condition:** They must not remind the recipient of their kindness. *We* indicates this, for it means: I have bestowed on you the livelihood out of which you give alms to the poor. As you are giving some of what belongs to Me, you cannot put the recipient under obligation.

**Fourth condition:** They must give to those who will spend it only for their livelihood. *They give as sustenance* points to this.

**Fifth condition:** They must give it for God's sake. *We have bestowed on them* states this. It means: You are giving out of My property, and so must give in My name.

Together with those conditions, the word *what* signifies that whatever God bestows is part of one's sustenance or livelihood. Thus believers must give out of whatever they have. For example, a good word, some help, advice, and teaching are all included in the meaning of *rizq* (sustenance) and *sadaqa* (alms). *What (ma)* has a general meaning and is not restricted here. Thus it includes whatever God has bestowed.

This short sentence contains and suggests a broad range of meaning for alms and offers it to our understanding. The word order of the Qur'an's sentences has many similar aspects, and the words have a wide range of relationships with one another. The same is true for the relationships between sentences, as seen in:

• *Surat al-Ikhlas*, which is as follows:

> Say: He is God, (He is) One. God is the Eternally-Besought-of-All. He did not beget, nor was He begotten. There is none comparable to Him. (112:1-5)

This short *sura* has six sentences, three positive and three negative, which prove and establish six aspects of Divine Unity and reject and negate six types of associating partners with God. Each sentence has two meanings: one *a priori* (functioning as a cause or proof) and the other *a posteriori* (functioning as an effect or result). That means that the *sura* contains 66 *suras*, each made up of six sentences. One is either a premise or a proposition, and the others are arguments for it. For example:

> Say: He is God, because He is One, because He is the Eternally-Besought-of-All, because He did not beget, because He was not begotten, because there is none comparable to Him.

Also:

> Say: There is none comparable to Him, because He was not begotten, because He did not beget, because He is the Eternally-Besought-of-All, because He is One, because He is God.

Also:

> He is God, therefore He is One, therefore He is the Eternally-Besought-of-All, therefore He did not beget, therefore He was not begotten, therefore there is none comparable unto Him.

- From *Surat al-Baqara*:

> Alif Lam Mim. That is the Book, there is no doubt in it; it is a guidance for the God-revering pious people. (2:1-2)

Each sentence has two meanings. One meaning is a proof for the others, and, through the other, their result. A composite design of miraculousness is woven from the 16 threads of relationship between them. This design was shown in my *Isharat al-I'jaz*. As explained in The Thir-teenth Word, it is as if each Qur'anic verse has an eye that sees most of the verses and a face that looks toward them. Given this, it extends to them the immaterial threads of relationship to weave a design of miraculousness. The beauty of composition is elaborated in *Isharat al-I'jaz*.

*SECOND POINT:* There is a wonderful eloquence in the Qur'an's meanings.

• Consider the following example: *All that is in the heavens and Earth glorifies God; and He is the All-Honored and Mighty, the All-Wise* (57:1, 59:1, 61:1).

To comprehend fully the eloquence in meanings, imagine that you are living in the desert of pre-Islamic Arabia. At a time when everything is enveloped by the darkness of ignorance and heedlessness and wrapped in the evil of "lifeless" nature, you hear from the Qur'an's heavenly tongue: *All that is in the heavens and Earth glorifies God or The seven heavens and Earth and those in them glorify Him* (17:44), or similar verses.

You will see how, in people's mind, those motionless corpse-like entities acquire a purposeful existence at the sound of: *All that is in the heavens and Earth glorifies God*, and being so raised, recite His Names. At the cry and light of *glorifies Him*, the stars, until then lifeless lumps of fire in the dark sky, appear in their understanding as wisdom-displaying words and truth-showing lights in the sky's recitation, the land and sea as tongues of praise, and each plant and animal as a word of glorification.

- From *Surat al-Rahman*:

> O company of jinn and humanity. If you can penetrate and pass beyond the spheres of the heavens and Earth, then penetrate and pass beyond (them). You will not penetrate and pass beyond them save with an authority. Which then of the blessings of your Lord do you deny? There will be sent on you a flash of fire, and smoke, and no help will you have, which then of the blessings of your Lord do you deny? (55:33-36)

> Verily, We have adorned the skies nearest the Earth with lamps, and made them missiles (to drive away) the devils. (67:5)

Listen to these verses, which are discussed in The Fifteenth Word, and pay attention to their meaning. They say:

O humanity and jinn. You are arrogant and refractory despite your impotence and wretchedness, rebellious and obstinate despite your weakness and destitution. If you do not want to obey My commands, pass beyond—if you can—the boundaries of My Kingdom. How dare you disobey a King Whose commands are obeyed by stars, moons, and suns as if they were trained soldiers ever ready to carry out their commander's commands. You rebel against a Majestic Ruler Who has such mighty and obedient soldiers that, supposing your satans were to resist, they could stone them to death with mountain-like cannonballs. Your ingratitude causes you to rebel in the Kingdom of a Majestic Sovereign Who has among His forces those that could hurl down upon you mountain-sized or even Earth-sized stars or flaming missiles, if you were unbelievers of that size, and rout you. Moreover, you infringe upon a law to which such beings are bound: If it were necessary, they could hurl the Earth in your face and rain down upon you stars as though missiles by God's leave.

Compare the force and eloquence in the meaning of other verses and their elevated style with these.

*THIRD POINT:* The Qur'an has unique, original styles that are both novel and convincing. Its styles, which still preserve their originality, freshness, and "bloom of youth," do not imitate and cannot be imitated. To cite a few examples:

• The *muqatta'at*:

The cipher-like *muqatta'at*, the disjunct, individual letters (e.g., *Alif-Lam-Mim, Alif-Lam-Ra, Ta-Ha, Ya-Sin, Ha-Mim,* and *'Ayn-Sin-Qaf,* with which some *sura*s begin), contain five or six gleams of miraculousness. For example, they comprise half of each category of the well-known categories of letters—emphatic, whispered, stressed, soft, labiolinguals, and *kalkale* (*ba, jim, dal, ta, qaf*). Taking more than half from the "light" letters and less than half from the "heavy" letters, neither of which are divisible, the Qur'an has halved every category.

Although it is possible to halve all categories, existing together one within the other, in one out of 200 probable ways, taking half from each category cannot be the work of a human mind or chance. Together with these disjunct letters at the beginning of certain *suras* as Divine ciphers displaying five or six further gleams of miraculousness like this, scholars well-versed in the mysteries of letters, as well as exacting, saintly scholars, have drawn many mysterious conclusions and discovered such truths that they consider these letters to form a most brilliant miracle. Since I cannot discover and show their secrets as clearly, I refer readers to the five or six gleams of their miraculousness explained in *Isharat al-I'jaz*.

I now discuss briefly the Qur'anic styles followed in its *sura*s, aims, verses, sentences and phrases, and words.

• Consider *Surat al-Naba'*:

*Surat al-Naba'* describes the Last Day and the Resurrection, as well as Paradise and Hell, in such an original and unique style that it convinces the heart that each Divine act and the work of Divine Lordship in this world proves the Hereafter's coming and all its aspects. In the interest of space, I mention only a few points.

At the start of the *sura*, it proves the Day of Judgment by:

> I have made Earth a beautiful cradle spread out for you, and the mountains bulwarks of your houses and lives full of treasures. I have created you in pairs, loving and familiar with each other, I have made the night a coverlet for your repose, the daytime the arena in which to gain your livelihood, and the sun an illuminating and heating lamp, and from the clouds I send down water as if they were

> a spring producing the water of life. I create easi-
> ly and in a short time from the one, same water all
> the flowering and fruit-bearing things which bear
> all your sustenance. Since this is so, the Last Day,
> which is the Day of Final Judgment, awaits you. It
> is not difficult for Us to bring about that Day. (78:6-
> 17—not exactly translated but interpreted [Tr.])

Following in the same strain, the *sura* implicitly proves that on the Last Day the mountains
will be moved and become as a mirage, the heavens rent asunder, Hell made ready, and the people
of Paradise given gardens and orchards. It means:
"Since He does all these things before your eyes
on Earth and mountains, He will do their likes in
the Hereafter."

In other words, the mountains mentioned at the
*sura*'s beginning have some relationship with the
Hereafter's mountains, and the gardens with the
gardens mentioned at the *sura*'s end and with those
in the Hereafter. Study other points from the same
view, and see how elevated its style really is.

• From *Surat Al-'Imran*:

> Say: O God, the Owner of Sovereignty: You give
> sovereignty to whom You will and You withdraw
> sovereignty from whom You will. You exalt whom

You will and You abase whom You will. In Your hand is the good. Surely You are powerful over all things. You cause the night to pass into the day, and You cause the day to pass into the night; You bring forth the living from the dead, and You bring the dead from the living. And You give sustenance to whom You will without measure. (3:26-27)

The Divine acts and operations in this world, the Divine manifestations in the alternation of day and night, the Lordship's control of the seasons and acts in life and death, and the world's changes, renewals, transformations, and convulsions are expressed in such a vivid and elevated style that it captivates the minds of the attentive. Since a little attention is enough to see this brilliant, elevated, and comprehensive style, I will go no further.

• From *Surat al-Inshiqaq*:

When heaven is split asunder and heeds (the command) of its Lord in submission, as in truth it must. And when Earth is leveled, and casts out all that is in it and becomes empty, and heeds (the command) of its Lord in submission, as in truth it must. (84:1-5)

These verses express in a most elevated style to what extent the heavens and Earth submit to and obey Almighty God's command. To accomplish and conclude a war—strategy, fighting, enrolling, and mobilizing soldiers, and so on—a commander-in-chief establishes two offices. After the fighting is over, he wants to use these offices for other business. However, the offices request him in the tongue of their staffs: "O commander, let us clean up and remove the bits and pieces of the former business, and then honor us with your presence." They do so, and then say to the commander: "Now we are at your command. Do what you wish, for whatever you do is right, good, and beneficial."

Similarly, the heavens and Earth were built as two arenas of testing and trial. Following the end of this period of trial for conscious beings, the heavens and Earth will expel the things connected with that trial at God's command. Then will they call: "O Lord, we are at Your command, so use us for whatever You wish. Our due is to obey You, for whatever You do is right and true." Based on this understanding, reflect upon the verses' elevated style and meaning.

- From *Sura Hud*:

> O Earth, swallow your water. O sky, withhold (your rain). And the water subsided. And the matter was

> accomplished. And (the Ark) came to rest upon
> (the mount) al-Judi, and it was said: Away with the
> wrongdoing folk. (11:44)

To point to a drop from the ocean of this verse's eloquence, I will show an aspect of its style through the mirror of an analogy. After victory, a commander orders one of his armies to cease fire and the other to remain where it is. He announces: "The job is well done. The enemy is defeated, and our flag is raised on the highest tower in the enemy's headquarters. Those aggressive wrongdoers have received what they deserved and have gone to the lowest of the low."

Similarly, the King Who has no equal ordered heaven and Earth to annihilate Noah's people. After they did so, He decreed:

> O Earth, swallow your water. O heaven, stop, for you
> have completed your duty. The water subsided. The
> ark came to rest upon the mountain as if setting up
> a tent. The wrongdoers received their due.

Consider how sublime this style is. The verse says that like two soldiers, heaven and Earth heed God's commands and obey Him. The style suggests that the universe is indignant and that the heavens and the Earth are furious with humanity's rebellion. Moreover, it warns humanity that its rebellion against the One Whose commands heaven and Earth obey is unreasonable and that people must not rebel. The verse expresses a very powerful restraint. In a few sentences, it describes a global event like the flood, with all its truths and results, in a concise, miraculous, and beautiful manner. Compare other drops of this ocean to this one.

Now consider the style apparent through the window of the Qur'an's words: *And for the moon We have determined mansions till it returns like an old shriveled date-stalk* (36:39). Look at like an old shriveled date-stalk. What a fine style it displays: One of the moon's mansions is the Pleiades. The verse compares the moon in its last quarter—the crescent—to an old shriveled date-stalk.

The comparison gives the impression that behind the sky's dark veil is a tree, one pointed shining stalk of which tears the veil and shows itself with the Pleiades like a cluster hanging from that stalk, and other stars like the glittering fruits of that hidden tree. If you have taste, you will appreciate what a proper, beautiful, fine, and noble style this is, especially for desert-dwellers whose most important means of livelihood is the date palm.

- From *Sura Ya Sin*:

> And the sun runs its course to a resting place destined. (36:38)

The expression *runs its course* is a noble image. By reminding us of Divine Power's systematic, magnificent, free acts and operations in alternating day and night as well as summer and winter, it makes the Maker's might and greatness understandable, turns one's attention to the Eternally-Besought-of-All's messages inscribed on the season's pages by the Pen of Power, and makes known the Creator's Wisdom.

By using *lamp* in *He has made the sun a lamp* (71:16), the Qur'an opens a window on a particular meaning: This world is a palace, its contents are humanity's and other living things' food and necessities of life, and a lamp (the sun) illuminates it. By making the Maker's magnificence and the Creator's favors comprehensible in this way, the sentence provides a proof for God's Unity and declares the sun (which the polytheists of that time viewed as the most significant and brightest deity) a lifeless object, a lamp subdued for the benefit of living beings.

In *lamp*, the verse signifies the Creator's mercy in His Lordship's might and greatness, reminds us of His favor in His Mercy's vastness, suggests His munificence in His Sovereignty's magnificence, and thereby proclaims His One-ness. It also teaches that a lifeless, subjected lamp is unworthy of worship. By indicating Almighty God's systematic, amazing acts in alternating night and day as well as winter and summer, it suggests the vast Power of the Maker, Who executes His Lordship independently.

Thus the verse deals with the sun and moon in a way to turn our attention to the pages of day and night, summer and winter, and the lines of events inscribed on them. The Qur'an mentions the sun not in its own name but in the name of the One Who has made it shining. It ignores the sun's physical nature, which does not benefit us, and draws our attention to its essential duties: to function as a wheel or spring for the delicate order of Divine creation and making, and as a shuttle for the harmony of Divine design in what the Eternal Designer weaves with the threads of night and day. When you compare other Qur'anic words with these, you see that each word, even if common, is a key to the treasury of fine meanings.

In sum, the vividness and extraordinariness of the Qur'an's styles sometimes entranced a Bedouin with one phrase, who would then prostrate without even being a Muslim. Once *Proclaim openly and insistently what you are commanded* (15:94) engendered this very reaction. When asked if he had become a Muslim, he answered: "No. I prostrate before the phrase's eloquence."

*FOURTH POINT:* The Qur'an's wording is extraordinarily fluent and pure. As it is extraordinarily eloquent when expressing meaning, so also it is wonderfully fluent and pure in wording and word arrangement. One proof of this is that it does not bore the senses; rather, it gives them pleasure, even if recited thousands of times. A child can memorize it easily. Seriously ill people, even if troubled by a few words of ordinary speech nearby, feel relief and comfort upon hearing it. It gives dying people's ears and minds the same taste and pleasure as that left by Zamzam water in their mouths and on their palates.

The Qur'an does not bore the senses; rather, it feeds the heart, gives power and wealth to the mind, functions as water and light for the spirit, and cures the soul's illnesses. We never tire of eating bread, but might tire of eating the same fruit every day. Similarly, reciting or listening to the Qur'an's pure truth and guidance does not bore us.

The Quraysh[23] sent one of its eloquent leaders to listen to the Qur'an. When he returned, he said: "It is so sweet and pleasing that no human tongue can resemble it. I know poets and soothsayers very well. The Qur'an is not like any of their work. We should describe it as sorcery so that it may not deceive our followers." Even its most hardened enemies admired its fluency and eloquence.

It would take too long to explain such things. One who looks at the arrangement of the letters in:

> Then, after grief, He sent down security for you, as slumber overcame a party of you. While another party lay troubled on their own account, moved by wrong suspicions of God, the suspicion of ignorance. They said: "Have we any part in the affair?" Say: "The affair wholly belongs to God." They hide within themselves [a thought] which they reveal

---

[23] The Quraysh was the Prophet's tribe.

> not to you, saying: "Had we had any part in the affair we would not have been slain here." Say: "Even though you had been in your houses, those appointed to be slain would have gone forth to the places where they were to fall. [All this was] in order that God might try what is in your breasts and prove what is in your hearts. God knows what is hidden in the breasts [of people]." (3:154)

will see the miraculousness brought about by the letters' extraordinary arrangement.

Such an arrangement, subtle relationship, delicate harmony and composition show that the verse is not the work of a person or chance. Such an order may be for other unknown purposes. Since the letters are arranged according to a certain system, there must be a mysterious order and illustrious coherence in the choice and arrangement of words, sentences, and meanings. Those who notice and understand it will remark: "What wonders God wills. How wonderfully God has made them."

*FIFTH POINT:* The Qur'an's expressions contain a superiority, power, sublimity, and magnificence. Its fluent, eloquent, and pure composition and word order, as well as eloquent meanings, and original and unique styles, lead to an evident excellence in its explanations. Truly, in all categories of expression and address, its expositions are of the highest degree.

For example: The expressions in *Surat al-Insan*, one of many examples of exhorting and encouraging good deeds, are most pleasing, like the water of a river of Paradise, and as sweet as the fruits of Paradise.

Aimed at deterrence and threat, its explanations at the beginning of *Surat al-Ghashiya* produce an effect like lead boiling in misguided people's ears, fire burning in their brains, Zaqqum scalding their palates, Hellfire assaulting their faces, and a bitter, thorny tree in their stomachs. That Hell, an "official" charged with torturing, tormenting, and demonstrating the Divine Being's threats, roars and nearly bursts with rage and fury (67:7-8), shows how dreadful and awesome that Being's powers of deterrence and threat are.

In the category of praise, the Qur'anic explanations in the five *sura*s beginning with *All praise be to God*[24] are brilliant like the sun, adorned like stars, majestic like the heavens and Earth, lovely like angels, full of the tenderness and compas-

---

[24] Namely, *al-Fatiha, al-An'am, al-Kahf, al-Saba', and al-Fatir.*

sion shown to the young in this world, and beautiful like Paradise. As for censure and restraint, consider: *Would any of you like to eat the flesh of his dead brother?* (49:12). It induces a heart-felt aversion to backbiting, reprimands the backbiter with six degrees of reprimand, and restrains him or her with six degrees of severity.

The initial *hamza* (in the original Arabic) is interrogative. This sense penetrates the entire sentence like water, so that each word in effect asks: "Do you not have enough intelligence to ask, answer, and discriminate between good and bad, to perceive how abominable this thing is?" *Like* asks: "Is your heart, with which you love and hate, so corrupted that you love such a repugnant thing?" *Any of you* asks: "What has happened to your sense of social relationship and civilization, which derive their liveliness from collectivity, that you accept something so poisonous to social life?"

*To eat the flesh* asks: "What has happened to your sense of humanity, that you tear your friend to pieces with your teeth like a wild animal?" *Of his brother* asks: "Do you have no human tenderness, no sense of kinship? How can you sink your teeth into an innocent person tied to you by numerous links of brotherhood? Or do you have no intelligence, and so senselessly bite into your own limbs?" *Dead* asks: "Where is your conscience? Is your nature so corrupt that you can engage in cannibalism although your brother deserves great respect?"

Thus slander and backbiting are repugnant to one's intelligence, heart, humanity, conscience, human nature, and religious and national brotherhood. This verse condemns backbiting in six degrees very concisely, and restrains people from it in six miraculous ways.

As for proving and demonstration, consider:

> Look, therefore, at the prints of God's mercy: how He revives Earth after its death. Indeed, He it is Who revives the dead (in the same way), and He is powerful over all things. (30:50)

This verse is such a wonderful proof of the Resurrection that no better proof is conceivable.

The annual spring resurrection of countless plants and animals that died during the previous autumn and winter contains infinite examples of resurrection.[25] The verse states that the One Who

---

[25] In the Ninth Truth of The Tenth Word and in the Fifth Gleam of The Twenty-second Word.

does these things can raise the dead with ease after destroying the world. Since it is the stamp of the One of Unity to inscribe on the page of Earth countless species with the Pen of His Power, one within the other without confusion, together with proving Divine Oneness like the sun, the verse shows the Resurrection as clearly as sunrise and sunset. The Qur'an uses *how* to refer to the way of Resurrection, and describes it in many other *sura*s.

Also, in *Sura Qaf* (50), the Qur'an proves the Resurrection in a brilliant, beautiful, lovely, and elevated manner of expression. Replying to the unbelievers' denial that decomposed bones can come to life once again, it declares:

> Have they not then observed the sky above them, how We have constructed it and beautified it, and how there are no rifts therein? And Earth We have spread out, and have flung firm hills therein, and have caused every lively kind to grow therein, a sight and a reminder for every penitent servant. And We send down from the sky blessed water whereby We give growth to gardens and the grain of crops, and lofty date-palms with ranged clusters, provision for people; and therewith We revive a dead land. Even so will be the resurrection of the dead. (50:6-11)

Truly, the manner of its exposition flows like water, glitters like stars and, just as dates give to the body, gives pleasure, delight, and nourishment to the heart.

A most delightful examples of proof and demonstration is: *Ya Sin. By the Wise Qur'an. Certainly you are among those sent (as Messengers of God)* (36:1-3). This oath points out that the proof of Muhammad's Messengership is so certain and true that an oath can be sworn upon it. In other words: "You are the Messenger, for the Qur'an, the truth and word of God, is in your hand. It contains true wisdom and bears the seal of miraculousness."

Another such concise and miraculous example is:

> (Humanity) asked: "Who will revive these bones when they have rotted away?" Say: "He will revive them Who built them at the first; He has absolute knowledge of every creation." (36:77-78)

As explained elsewhere, one who reassembles a huge, dispersed army in a day can certainly gather, through a trumpet call, a battalion dispersed for rest and then line the soldiers up in their previous positions.[26] Not believing this is irrational.

---

[26] In the Third Comparison of the Ninth Truth of The Tenth Word.

Similarly, an All-Powerful, All-Knowing One can assemble all living beings' atoms, regardless of location, by: *"Be, and it is"* (2:117) with perfect orderliness and the balance of wisdom, and make from them bodies having the most delicate senses and keenest faculties. Each spring He creates infinite army-like animate species on Earth. If He can do this, why do you think He cannot reassemble all of a formerly living entity's atoms and raise it in a new body by a blow of Israfil's Trumpet?

As for guidance, the Qur'an is so affective, penetrating, tender, and touching that its verses uplift the spirit with ardor, the heart with delight, the intellect with curiosity, and the eyes with tears. Just one example shows this:

> Then your hearts became hardened thereafter and were like stones, or even harder; for there are stones from which rivers come gushing, and others split, so that water issues from them, and others crash down in the fear of God. God is not heedless of the things you do. (2:74)

This verse, addressed to the Children of Israel, means: "Even a hard rock cried tears like a spring from its twelve 'eyes' when it saw Moses' miracle, and yet your eyes remained dry and your hearts hard and unfeeling. What has happened to you?" Since the verse's meaning was elaborated elsewhere, I will not discuss it here.[27]

As for silencing and overcoming in argument, consider the following verse:

> If you are in doubt concerning what We have sent down on Our servant, then bring a sura like it and call your helpers and witnesses, other than God, if you are truthful. (2:23)

The verse, directed to humanity and jinn, briefly means:

> If you think a human being wrote the Qur'an, let one of your unlettered people, as Muhammad is unlettered, produce something similar. If he cannot, send your most famous writers or scholars. If they cannot, let them work together and call upon all their history, "deities," scientists, philosophers, sociologists, theologians, and writers to produce something similar. If they cannot, let them try— leaving aside the miraculous and inimitable aspects

---

[27] In the First Station of The Twentieth Word. These are: *When We said unto the angels, "Prostrate before Adam, they fell prostrate," all save Iblis* (2:34); *God commands you to sacrifice a cow* (2:67); *and Then your hearts became hardened thereafter and were like stones, or even yet harder* (2:74).

of its meaning—to produce a work of equal eloquence in word order and composition.

By: *Then bring 10 suras like it, contrived* (11:13), the Qur'an means:

> What you write does not have to be true. But if you still cannot match the Qur'an's length, produce only 10 chapters. If you cannot do that, produce only one chapter. If you cannot do that, produce only a short chapter. If you cannot do that—which you cannot—although such inability will put your honor, religion, nationality, lives, and property at risk, you will die humiliated. Moreover, as stated in: *Then fear the Fire, whose fuel is people and stones* (2:24), you and your idols will spend eternity in Hell. Having understood your eight degrees of inability, what else can you do but admit eight times that the Qur'an is a miracle?

As for silencing, consider: There cannot be and is no need for any other exposition after that of the Qur'an, as well as:

> Therefore remind. By Your Lord's blessing you are not a soothsayer, neither possessed. Or do they say: "He is a poet for whom we await what fate will bring?" Say: "Wait. I shall be waiting with you." Or do their intellects bid them to do this? Or are they an insolent, rebellious people? Or do they say:

"He has invented it?" Nay, but they do not believe.
Then let them bring a discourse like it, if they speak
truly. Or were they created out of nothing? Or are
they the creators? Or did they create the heavens
and Earth? Nay, but they do not have sure belief.
Or are your Lord's treasuries in their keeping? Or
are they the watching registrars? Or do they have
a ladder whereon they listen? Then let any of them
that listened bring a clear authority. Or does He have
daughters, and they sons? Or do you ask them for
a wage, and so they are weighed down with debt?
Or is the Unseen in their keeping, and so they are
writing it down? Or do they intend a plot? But those
who disbelieve, are they the outwitted? Or have they
a god, other than God? Glory be to God, above that
which they associate. (52:29-43)

I will discuss only one of the countless truths
found in these verses to show how the Qur'an
silences it opponents: Through 15 questions introduced by *Or*, which express a rejection and impossibility, it silences all opponents, ends all doubt,
and makes misguidance impossible. It rends all
veils under which they may hide and discloses their
fallacies. Each question exposes the fallacy, remains
silent where a fallacy is evident, or refutes briefly
(and in more detail elsewhere) the unbelievers'
assertion. For example, it refers their assertion that
the Prophet is a poet to: *We have not taught him*

*poetry; it is not seemly for him* (36:69), and their claim in the last section finds its answer in: *Were there gods in them (Earth and the heavens) other than God, they would surely go to ruin* (21:22).

In the beginning, it says: "Relay the Divine Commandments. You are not a soothsayer, for their words are confused and consist of conjecture. You speak the truth with absolute certainty and are not possessed. Even your enemies testify to your perfect intellect." Or do they say: "He is a poet. We will wait to see what happens." Say to them: "Wait, and I shall also be waiting." The great and brilliant truths you bring are free of poetic fancy and artificial embellishment.

Or do their intellects bid them to do this? Or, like senseless philosophers, do they consider their own intellects sufficient and so refuse to follow you? Any sound intellect requires following you, for whatever you say is reasonable. However, human intellect is unable to produce a like of it and grasp it by itself. Or are they insolent and rebellious? Or, like rebellious wrongdoers, is their denial due to their non-submission to truth? Everybody knows the end of such leaders of mutinous wrongdoers as Pharaoh and Nimrod.

Or do they say: "He has invented it." They do not believe, and, like lying and unscrupulous hypocrites, accuse you of inventing the Qur'an. Until this time, however, they knew you as the most trustworthy among them and even called you Muhammad the Trustworthy. They have no intention to believe. Otherwise they must find a human work similar to the Qur'an.

Or were they created out of nothing? Or, like those philosophers who see existence as absurd and purposeless, do they regard themselves as purposeless, without a Creator, and left to themselves? Are they blind? Do they not see that the universe is embellished with instances of wisdom and fruitfulness, that everything has duties and obeys Divine commandments?

Or are they the creators? Or, like materialists who are each like a Pharaoh, do they imagine themselves self-existent and self-subsistent, able to create whatever they need? Is this why they refuse belief and worship? It seems that they consider themselves creators. But one who creates one thing must be able to create everything. Self-conceit and vanity have made them so foolish that they suppose such an impotent one to be absolutely powerful. They are so devoid of humanity and reason that they have fallen lower than animals and inanimate objects. So do not be grieved by their denial.

Or did they create the heavens and Earth? No, for they have no sure belief. Or, like those who deny the Creator, do they deny God and so ignore the Qur'an? If so, let them deny the existence of the heavens and Earth or claim to be their creators, so that all can see their complete lack of reason. The proofs of Divine Existence and Unity are as numerous as stars and as many as flowers. Such people have no intention of acquiring sure belief and accepting the truth. Otherwise, how can they say that this Book of the Universe, in each letter of which is inscribed a book, has no author when they know that a letter must have an author?

Or do they possess your Lord's treasuries? Or, like some misguided philosophers and Brahmans who deny Almighty God's free will, do they deny Prophethood and therefore belief in you? If so, let them deny all prints of wisdom, purpose, order, purposeful results, favors, and works of mercy seen throughout the universe. Let them manifest a deliberate choice and absolute will, as well as all the Prophets' miracles. Or let them claim to possess the treasuries of favors bestowed on all creatures, and show that they are not worthy of address. If this is so, do not feel sorrow for their denial.

Or are they watching registrars? Or, like the Mu'tazilites who made reason the absolute authority in judging matters, do they consider themselves overseers and inspectors of the Creator's work and desire to hold Him responsible? Never be disheartened and do not mind their denial, for it is vain. Or do they have a ladder whereon they listen? If so, let one of them bring a clear authority.

Or, like the soothsayers and spiritualists who follow jinn and Satan, do they imagine that they have discovered another route to the Unseen? Do they think they have a ladder by which to ascend to the heavens, which are closed to their satans? Is this why they deny your heavenly tidings? The denial of such people means nothing.

Or has He daughters and they sons? Or, like philosophers who associate partners with God (e.g., the Ten Intellects and the Masters of Species), the Sabeans (who ascribe a sort of divinity to heavenly objects and angels), or those who attribute sons to God Almighty, do they assert that angels are His daughters, despite the fact that such is contrary to the necessary existence of the Unique, Eternally Besought One, to His Unity and absolute independence, to His being the Eternally-Besought-of-All, and to the innocence and servanthood of the genderless angels? Do they consider angels their intercessors with God and therefore not follow you? Sexual relations ensure the multiplication, cooperation, and continuance of all contingent and mortal entities.

A great example is humanity, whose members are impotent, enamored with the world, and want to be succeeded by children. It is sheer foolishness to ascribe fatherhood to God, for His necessary and eternal Existence, absolute freedom from all physical qualities, exemption from multiplication and division, and absolute power make fatherhood unnecessary. Even more amazing is their saying that God has daughters, when they regard their own daughters as sources of shame. Given this, do not mind the denial of such people.

Or do you ask them for a wage and place them in debt? Or, like the rebellious and insolent, miserly and ambitious, do they find the commandments you convey unbearable and so avoid you? Do they not know that you expect your wage only from

God? They find it hard to receive the blessing of abundant wealth, and yet have to give one-tenth or one-fortieth of it to the poor. Do they oppose Islam so that they will not have to pay *zakat*?[28] Their denial is not worth answering, and they will be punished.

Or is the Unseen in their keeping? Are they writing it down? Or, like those who claim to have knowledge of the Unseen and those pseudo-intellectuals who imagine their guesses of future events to be certain, do they not like your tidings of the Unseen? Do they have books of the Unseen that refute your book of the Unseen?

If so, they mistakenly believe that the Unseen, which is only open to Messengers receiving Divine Revelation and cannot be entered by anyone on his or her own, is open to them and that they are just writing down the information they obtain from it. Do not be disheartened by the denial of such

---

[28] The obligatory amount of wealth that each adult and sane Muslim who can do so must give each year to any or all of the eight classes of people mentioned in 9:60. Its exact amount and who can receive it depends upon various factors. (Ed.)

conceited people, for the truths you bring will destroy their fancies in a very short time.

Or do they want to outwit you? Know that the unbelievers are outwitted. Or, like hypocrites and heretics, do they encourage others to join them in their unbelief or consider you a soothsayer, a magician, or one possessed? They are not truly human, and so you should not be disheartened by their denial and tricks. Rather, be more vigorous and strive harder, for their trickery only deceives themselves. Their apparent success in evil-doing is temporary, a gradual perdition prepared for them by God.

Or do have they a deity other than God? Glory be to God, above that which they associate. Or, like the Magians who believe in two deities (a creator of goodness and a creator of evil), and those who attribute everything to causality and make it a point of support for them, do they rely on false deities and argue with you? Do they consider themselves independent of you?

If they do, they are blind to the universe's perfect order and delicate coherence: *Were there deities in them (the heavens and Earth) other than God, they would surely go to ruin* (21:22). Two headmen or elders in a village, two governors in a town, or two sovereigns in a country would make order impossible. If God had partners, the universe's delicate order and harmony would be impossible. Since such people act completely contrary to reason, wisdom, common sense, and evident realities, do not let their denial cause you to abandon communicating the Divine Message.

So far, I have sought to summarize only one of the hundreds of jewels in such truth-laden verses. If I could show a few more of their jewels, you would conclude: "Each verse is a miracle."

The Qur'anic expositions in teaching and explaining are so wonderful, beautiful, and fluent that anyone can understand easily the most profound truths. The Qur'an of miraculous exposition teaches and explains many profound and subtle truths so clearly and directly that it neither offends human sensibility nor opposes generally held opinions. Rather, such exposition conforms with what is familiar to us.

Just as one uses appropriate words when addressing a child, the Qur'an, "the Divine address to the human mind," uses a style appropriate to its audience's level. It uses allegories, parables, and comparisons to makes the most difficult Divine truths and mysteries easily understood by even the most common, unlettered person. For example: *The Most Merciful One has settled Himself on the Supreme Divine Throne* (20:5) shows Divine Lord-ship as though it were a kingdom, and the aspect of His Lordship administering the universe as though He were a King seated on His Sovereignty's throne and exercising His rule.

The Qur'an, the word of the Majestic Creator of the universe issuing from His Lordship's highest degree of manifestation, surpasses all other degrees. It guides those who rise to those degrees, and passes through 70,000 veils to illuminate each. Radiating enlightenment to all levels of understanding and intelligence, it pours out its meaning, regardless of people's ability and scientific level, and keeps its infinite freshness and delicacy. It continues to teach all people in an easy yet most skillful and comprehensible way, and convinces them of its truth. Wherever you look in it, you will find a gleam of its miraculousness.

In short, when a Qur'anic phrase like *All praise be to God* is recited, it fills up the ear of a tiny fly as well as that of a mountain (a cave). Likewise, just as its meanings fully saturate the greatest intellects, the same words satisfy the smallest intellects. The Qur'an calls all levels of humanity and jinn to belief and instructs them in the sciences of belief. Given this, the most unlettered person as well as the most distinguished member of the educated elite will follow and benefit from its lessons.

The Qur'an is such a heavenly table spread with intellectual and spiritual foods that beings of all levels of intellect, reason, heart, and spirit can find their sustenance and satisfy their appetites therein. Moreover, the Qur'an has many more treasures of meaning and truths that will be opened by future generations. The whole Qur'an is an example of this truth. All Muslims, regardless of profession, level of intelligence, or knowledge of God, declare: "The Qur'an teaches us in the best way."

## Second ray

This ray, the extraordinary comprehensiveness of the Qur'an, consists of five gleams.

**FIRST GLEAM:** This comes from the Qur'an's comprehensive wording, which was discussed in the previous Words, as well as in the verses whose meanings are quoted in this Word. As pointed out in the Traditions, each verse has outer and inner meanings, limits and a point of comprehension, as well as boughs, branches, and twigs.[29] Each phrase, word, letter, and diacritical point has many aspects. Each person who hears it receives his or her share through a different door.

• From *Surat al-Naba*:

> And the mountains as masts. (78:7)

means: "I have made mountains like masts and stakes for your Earth." Ordinary people see mountains as if driven into the ground and thank the Creator for the resulting benefits and bounties. Poets imagine Earth as a ground on which the heavens' dome is pitched, in a sweeping arc, as a mighty blue tent adorned with electric lamps. Seeing mountains skirting the heavens' base as tent pegs, they worship the Majestic Creator in amazement.

Desert-dwelling literary people imagine Earth as a vast desert, and its mountain chains as many nomads' tents. They see them as if the soil were stretched over high posts and as if the posts' pointed tips had raised the "cloth" of the soil, which they

---

[29] Ibn Hibban, *Sahih*, 1:146; al-Munawi, *Fayd al-Qadir*, 3:54.

see as the home for countless creatures. They prostrate in amazement before the Majestic Creator, Who placed and set up such imposing and mighty things so easily.

Geographers with a literary bent view Earth as a ship sailing in the ocean of air or ether, and mountains as masts giving balance and stability to the ship. Before the All-Powerful One of Perfection, Who has made Earth like a well-built orderly ship on which He makes us travel through the universe, they declare: "Glory be to You. How magnificent is Your creation."

Philosophers or historians of culture see Earth as a house, the pillar of whose life is animal life that, in turn, is supported by air, water, and soil (the conditions of life). Mountains are essential for these conditions, for they store water, purify the atmosphere by precipitating noxious gases, and preserve the ground from becoming a swamp and being overrun by the sea. Mountains also are treasuries for other necessities of human life. In perfect reverence, they praise the Maker of Majesty and Munificence, Who has made these great mountains as pillars for Earth, the house of our life, and appointed them as keepers of our livelihood's treasuries.

Naturalist scientists say: "Earth's quakes and tremors, which are due to certain underground formations and fusions, were stabilized with the emergence of mountains. This event also stabilized Earth's axis and orbit. Thus its annual rotation is not affected by earthquakes. Its wrath and anger is quietened by its coursing through mountain vents." They would come to believe and declare: "There is a wisdom in everything God does."

• From *Surat al-Anbiya'*:

> The heavens and Earth were of one piece; then We parted them. (21:30)

To learned people who have not studied materialist philosophy, *of one piece* means that when the heavens were clear and without clouds, and Earth was dry, lifeless, and unable to give birth, God opened the heavens with rain and the soil with vegetation, and created all living beings through a sort of marriage and impregnation. Such people understand that everything is the work of such an All-Powerful One of Majesty that Earth's face is His small garden, and all clouds veiling the sky's face are sponges for watering it. They prostrate before His Power's tremendousness.

To exacting sages, it means: "In the beginning, the heavens and Earth were a formless mass, each consisting of matter like wet dough without produce or creatures. The All-Wise Creator separated them and rolled them out and, giving each a comely shape and beneficial form, made them the origins of multiform, adorned creatures." These sages are filled with admiration at His Wisdom's comprehensiveness.

Modern philosophers or scientists understand that the solar system was fused like a mass of dough. Then the All-Powerful and Self-Subsistent One rolled it out and placed the planets in their respective positions. He left the sun where it was and brought Earth here. Spreading soil over its face, watering it with rain, and illuminating it with sunlight, He made the world habitable and placed us on it. These people are saved from the swamp of naturalism, and declare: "I believe in God, the One, the Unique."

• From *Sura Ya Sin*:

> The sun runs its course to a resting place destined. (36:38)

The particle *li* (written as the single letter *lam*), translated here as "to," expresses the meanings of "toward," "in," and "for." Ordinary people read it as "toward" and understand that the sun, which is a moving lamp providing light and heat, one day will reach its place of rest and, ending its journey, assume a form that will no longer benefit them. Thinking of the great bounties that the Majestic Creator bestows through the sun, they declare: "All glory be to God. All praise be to God."

Learned people also read *li* as "toward," but see the sun as both a lamp and a shuttle for the Lord's textiles woven in the loom of spring and summer, as an ink-pot whose ink is light for the letters of the Eternally-Besought-of-All inscribed on the pages of night and day. Reflecting on the world's order, of which the sun's apparent movement is a sign and to which it points, they declare before the All-Wise Maker's art: "What wonders God has willed," before His Wisdom: "May God bless it," and prostrate.

For geographer–philosophers, *li* means "in" and suggests that the sun orders and propels its system through Divine command and with a spring-like movement on its own axis. Before the Majestic

Creator, Who created and set in order a mighty clock like the solar system, they exclaim in perfect amazement and admiration: "All great-ness and power is God's," abandon materialistic philosophy, and embrace the wisdom of the Qur'an.

Precise and wise scholars consider *li* to be causal *and* adverbial. They understand that since the All-Wise Maker operates behind the veil of apparent causality, He has tied the planets to the sun by His law of gravity and causes them to revolve with distinct but regular motions according to His universal wisdom. To produce gravity, He has made the sun's movement on its axis an apparent cause. Thus *a resting place* means that "the sun moves in the place determined for it for the order and stability of its own (solar) system."

Like the Divine laws, that motion produces heat, heat produces force, and force produces gravity. The sun is a law of Divine Lordship. On understanding such an instance of wisdom from a single letter of the Qur'an, wise scholars declare: "All praise be to God. True wisdom is found in the Qur'an. Human philosophy is worth almost nothing."

The following idea occurs to poets from this *li* and the stability mentioned: "The sun is a light-diffusing tree, and the planets are its moving fruits. But unlike trees, the sun is shaken so that the fruits do not fall. If it were not shaken, they would fall and be scattered." They also may imagine the sun to be a leader of a circle reciting God's Names, ecstatically reciting in the circle's center and leading the others to recite. Elsewhere, I expressed this meaning as follows:

> The sun is a fruit-bearing tree;
> it is shaken so that its
> travelling fruits do not fall.
> If it rested, no longer shaken,
> the attraction would cease, and those
> attracted to it would weep through space.

• From *Surat al-Baqara*:

They are those who will prosper. (2:5)

This general verse does not specify how they will prosper. Thus each person may find what they pursue in it. The sense is compact so that it may be comprehensive. People seek to be saved from the Fire, enter Paradise, or acquire eternal happiness. Others seek God's good pleasure or the vision of God. In many places, the Qur'an neither narrows nor specifies the sense, for it can express many meanings by leaving certain things unsaid.

By not specifying in what way they will prosper, it means: "O Muslims, good tidings! O God-fearing one, you will be saved from Hell. O righteous one, you will enter Paradise. O one with knowledge of God, you will gain God's good pleasure. O lover of God, you will be rewarded with the vision of God."

• From *Sura Muhammad*:

> Know that there is no god but God, and ask forgiveness for your error. (47:19)

This verse has so many aspects and degrees that all saints consider themselves in need of it and derive from it a fresh meaning and spiritual nourishment appropriate to their ranks. This is because "God" is the Divine Being's all-comprehensive Name, and thus it contains as many affirmations of Divine Unity as the number of the Divine Names: There is no provider but He, no creator but He, no merciful one but He, and so on.

The story of Moses has thousands of benefits and pursues many purposes, such as calming and consoling the Prophet, threatening unbelievers, condemning hypocrites, and reproaching Jews. Thus it is repeated in several *sura*s to stress different aspects. Although all purposes are relevant in each place, only one is the main purpose.

*QUESTION:* How do you know the Qur'an contains and intends all those meanings?

*ANSWER:* As the Qur'an is an eternal discourse speaking to and teaching humanity at all levels and times, it contains, intends, and alludes to all of those meanings. In my *Isharat al-I'jaz*, I use Arabic grammatical rules, as well as the principles of rhetoric, semantics, and eloquence, to prove that the Qur'an's words include and intend various meanings. According to Muslim jurists' consensus and interpretations, Qur'anic interpreters, and scholars of religious methodology, all aspects and meanings understood from the Qur'an can be considered among its meanings if they accord with Arabic's grammatical rules, Islam's principles, and the sciences of rhetoric, semantics, and eloquence.

The Qur'an has placed a sign, either literal or allusive, for each meaning according to its degree. If allusive, there is another sign from either the preceding or the following context, or another verse to point to the meaning. Thousands of Qur'anic commentaries prove its wording's extraordinary comprehensiveness. Interested readers can refer to my *Isharat al-I'jaz* for a more extensive (yet still partial) discussion.

**SECOND GLEAM:** This relates to the Qur'an's extraordinarily comprehensive meaning. In addition to bestowing the sources for exacting jurists, the illuminations of those seeking knowledge of God, the ways of those trying to reach God, the paths of perfected human beings, and the schools of truth-seeking scholars from the treasuries of its meaning, the Qur'an always has guided them and illuminated their ways. All agree on this.

**THIRD GLEAM:** This relates to the extraordinary comprehensiveness of the knowledge contained in the Qur'an. Not only is its vast knowledge the source of countless sciences related to the Shari'a, truth (*haqiqa*), and religious orders (*tariqa*), but the Qur'an also contains true wisdom and scientific knowledge of the Sphere of Contingencies (the material world), true knowledge of the Realm of Necessity (the Divine realm), and esoteric knowledge of the Hereafter. For examples, consider the previous Words, although they are only 25 drops from the oceans of the Qur'an's knowledge. Any errors in those Words come from my defective understanding.

**FOURTH GLEAM:** This relates to the Qur'an's extraordinarily comprehensive subject matter. It deals with humanity and its duties, the universe and its Creator, the heavens and Earth, this world and the next, and the past, future, and eternity. It explains all essential matters related to our creation and life, from correct ways of eating and sleeping to issues of Divine Decree and Will, from the universe's creation in 6 days to the functions of winds alluded to in such oaths as: *By the (winds) sent forth* (77:1) and *By the (winds) that scatter* (51:1).

It discusses so many other topics: from God's intervention in our heart and free will: *(God) stands between a person and his [her] heart* (8:24), and *But you will not unless God wills* (76:30) to His grasp of the heavens: *The heavens shall be rolled up in His "right hand"* (39:67); from Earth's flowers, grapes, and dates: *We made therein gardens of palms and vines* (36:34) to the astounding event described in: *When Earth is shaken with a mighty shaking* (99:1); from heaven's state during creation: *Then He comprehended in His design the sky when it was smoke* (41:11) to its splitting open and the stars being scattered in endless space; from building this world for testing and trial to its destruction; from the grave, the other world's first station, to the Resurrection, the Bridge, and eternal happiness in Paradise.

It also discusses the past, including:

> When your Lord took from the children of Adam, from their loins, their seed, and made them testify of themselves, (saying): "Am I not your Lord?" They said: "Yes, assuredly. We testify."—lest you should say on the Day of Resurrec-tion: "Of this, we were unaware" (7:172),

the creation of Adam's body and the struggle between his two sons, the Flood, the drowning of Pharaoh's people, and the Prophets' life-stories, to what will happen on the Day of Judgment: *When some faces shall be radiant, gazing upon their Lord* (75:22).

The Qur'an explains all such essential and important matters in a way befitting an All-Powerful One of Majesty, Who administers the universe like a palace, opens and closes the world and the Hereafter like two rooms, controls Earth like a garden and the heavens like a lamp-adorned dome, and in Whose sight the past and future are like day and night or two pages, and eternity like a point of present time.

Like a builder describing two houses he has built and listing what he will do, the Qur'an is—if one may express it—a list or program written in a suitable style for the One Who has built and administers the universe. The Qur'an says that it is the Word of the Creator of the universe. It contains no trace of artifice, pretence, or unnecessary trouble, and no strain of imitation, trickery, or deception. It does not pretend to speak in another's name. Like daylight announcing to be from the sun, with its absolutely genuine, pure, clear, solemn, original, and brilliant style, it declares: "I am the Word of the Creator of the universe."

Can the Qur'an belong to someone other than the Maker, the Bestower of Bounties, Who has decorated this world with the most original and invaluable works of art and filled it with the most pleasant bounties? It resonates throughout the world with cries of acclamation and commendation, litanies of praise and thanks, and has made Earth into a house where God's Names are recited, where God is worshipped and His works of art are studied in amazement. Where can the light illuminating the world be coming from, if not from the sun? Whose light can the Qur'an be, other than the Eternal Sun's, which has unveiled and illuminated the universe's meaning? Who could dare to produce a like of it?

It is inconceivable that the Artist Who decorated this world with the works of His art should not address humanity, who appreciates and commends that art. Since He knows and makes, He will speak. Since He speaks, He will speak through the Qur'an. How could God, the Lord of all dominion Who is not indifferent to a flower's formation, be indifferent to a Word resonating throughout His dominion? Could He allow others to appropriate it, thereby reducing it to futility and to nothing?

**FIFTH GLEAM:** This consists of five beams related to the Qur'an's comprehensive style and conciseness.

*FIRST BEAM:* The Qur'an is so wonderfully comprehensive in style that one *sura* may contain the whole ocean of the Qur'an in which the universe is contained. One verse may comprehend that *sura*'s treasury, as if most verses are small *sura*s and most *sura*s are little Qur'ans.

This miraculous conciseness is a great gift of Divine Grace with respect to guidance and easiness, for although everyone always needs the

Qur'an, not all people read it. So that they are not deprived of its blessings, each *sura* may substitute for a small Qur'an and each long verse for a short *sura*. Moreover, all people of spiritual discovery and scholars agree that the Qur'an is contained in *Surat al-Fatiha*, which is itself contained in the *basmala* (In the Name of God, the Merciful, the Compassionate).

*SECOND BEAM:* The Qur'an contains references to all knowledge needed by humanity.[30] Moreover, it gives people whatever they need, so that: *Take from the Qur'an whatever you wish, for whatever need you have* has been widely circulated among verifying scholars. Its verses are so comprehensive that the cure for any ailment and the answer for any need can be found therein. This must be so, for the Book that is the absolute guide of all perfected people who each day move forward in the way of God must be of that quality.

---

[30] Such as explanations, aspects, and varieties of true knowledge, commands and prohibitions, promises and threats, encouragement and deterrence, restraint and guidance, stories and parables, Divine knowledge and commands, natural sciences, and the rules and conditions of our personal, social, spiritual, and otherworldly lives.

*THIRD BEAM:* The Qur'an's expressions are concise but all-inclusive. Sometimes it mentions the first and last terms of a long series in a way that shows all of it; other times it includes in a word many explicit, implicit, allusive, or suggestive proofs of a cause.

• From *Surat al-Rum*:

> And of His signs is the creation of the heavens and Earth and the variety of your tongues and colors. (30:22)

By mentioning the universe's two-part creation—the creation of the heavens and Earth and the varieties of human languages and races—it suggests the creation and variety of all animate and inanimate beings as signs of Divine Unity. This also testifies to the All-Wise Maker's Existence and Unity, Who first created the heavens and Earth and then followed this with other links—from adorning the heavens with stars to populating Earth with animate creatures; from giving the sun, Earth, and moon regular orbits, as well as alternating day and night, to differentiating and individualizing speech and complexion in cases of extreme multiplication.

Since creating the vast heavens and Earth displays certain artistry and purposes, the artistry and purpose of a Maker Who founded universe on the heavens and Earth will be much more explicit in other parts of His creation. Thus, by manifesting what is concealed and concealing what is manifest, the verse displays an extremely beautiful conciseness.

Also, more probably than all other things in existence, the amazing purposeful system of differentiation clearly manifests a deliberate order. Although one may suppose this system to be determined by chance, the links of creation point to their Designer.

The evidence beginning six times with: *Of His signs from so glory be to God both in your evening hour and in your morning hour* (30:17), to *His is the highest comparison in the heavens and Earth; He is the All-Mighty, the All-Wise* (30:27), is a series of jewels, lights, miracles, and miraculous conciseness. I wish to show the diamonds in those treasures, but must postpone doing so.

• From *Sura Yusuf*:

> Then said the one who had been delivered, remembering after a time: "I will myself tell you its inter-

> pretation; so send me forth." "Joseph, you truthful
> man..." (12:45-46)

The narrative omits several events between *so send me forth* and *Joseph, you truthful man*: [So send me forth] to Joseph so that I may ask him about the dream's interpretation. They sent him. He came to the prison and said: [Joseph ...]. In such a way does the Qur'an narrate briefly and to the point without any loss of clarity.

• From *Sura Ya Sin*:

> Who has made fire for you out of the green tree.
> (36:80)

and, in the face of rebellious humanity's denial of the Resurrection:

> Who shall quicken the bones when they are rotted
> away? (36:78)

The Qur'an says: "The One Who originated them shall quicken them. The One Who creates knows all aspects of all things. Moreover, the One Who made fire for you out of the green tree can quicken decayed bones." The part of the verse quoted deals with (and proves) the Resurrection from different viewpoints.

First, it reminds us of Divine favors. Since the Qur'an details them elsewhere, it only alludes to them here. It actually means: "You cannot escape or hide from the One Who made fire for you out of trees, causes them to give you fruits, provides you with grains and plants, has made Earth a lovely cradle containing all your provisions, and the world a beautiful palace containing whatever you require. You have not been created in vain and without purpose, and so you are not free or able to sleep in the grave eternally without being woken up."

Second, in pointing to a proof of the Resurrection, it uses the green tree to suggest: "O you who deny the Resurrection, look at trees. How can you deny the Power of the One Who quickens in spring innumerable trees that died and hardened in winter? By causing them to blossom, come into leaf and produce fruits, He exhibits three examples of the Resurrection on each tree." It points to another proof and means: "How can you deem it unlikely for One Who makes a refined and light-giving substance like fire out of hard, dark, and heavy trees? How can you say that He cannot give a fire-like life and a light-like consciousness to wood-like bones?"

It points out yet another proof: "Everything in the universe is subject to and depends on the decrees of the One Who creates fire when nomads rub two green tree branches together, and reconciles opposing natures to produce new things. How can you oppose Him and consider the Resurrection unlikely?" Moreover, it alludes to the well-known tree near which Prophet Moses received the first Revelation and suggests that Muhammad's cause and that of Moses are the same. Thus it refers indirectly to all Prophets' agreement on the same essential points and adds yet another meaning to the compact treasures of that word's meaning.

*FOURTH BEAM:* The Qur'an's conciseness is like offering the ocean in a pitcher. Out of mercy and courtesy for ordinary human minds, it shows the most comprehensive and universal principles and general laws through a particular event on a particular occasion. The following examples are only a few of many such concise examples:

- The explanation of three verses in the First Station of The Twentieth Word.

Several things are suggested. Teaching humanity the names of all things means that men and women were given the potential to obtain all knowledge and science; the angels' prostration before Adam and Satan's refusal to do so signify that most creatures have been placed at our disposal, while harmful beings (e.g., Satan and snakes) will not be so docile. Mentioning the Israelites' slaughtering of a cow means that cow worship (borrowed from Egypt and shown in the Israelites' adoration of the calf made for them by the Samiri: 20:85-88) was destroyed by Moses' knife. Mentioning that rivers gush forth from some rocks, that others split so that water issues from them, and that still others crash down in fear of God (2:74) states implicitly that subsurface rock strata allow subterranean veins of water to pass through them and that they had a role in Earth's origin.

• Each phrase and sentence of Moses' story points to and expresses a universal principle.

For example, in: *Haman, build for me a tower* (40:36), the Qur'an means: "Pharaoh ordered his minister Haman: 'Build a high tower for me. I will observe the heavens and try to find out through heavenly events whether there is a god such as Moses claims.'"

Through this particular event and by *tower*, the Qur'an alludes to a curious custom of the Pharaohs: Worshippers of nature who lived in a vast desert without mountains, believers in sorcery and reincarnation because of unbelief in God, they cherished a deep desire for mountains and claimed absolute sovereignty like that of Divine Lordship over people. To eternalize their names and fame, they built mountain-like pyramids for their mummified bodies.

• From *Sura Yunus*:

> So today We shall deliver you with your body. (10:92)

By mentioning Pharaoh's drowning, the Qur'an suggests: "Since all Pharaohs believed in reincarnation, they mummified their bodies to eternalize themselves. Thus their bodies have survived until now. Although not mummified, the body of the Pharaoh who drowned while pursuing Moses with his army, was found prostrate beside the Nile in the closing years of the nineteenth century. This is an explicit Qur'anic miracle, which foretold it centuries ago in the verse in question.

• From *Sura Yunus*:

> [T]he folk of Pharaoh who were visiting you with evil chastisement, slaughtering your sons and sparing your women [to use them]. (2:49)

This verse mentions the Pharaohs' evils and cruelties to the Israelites. It also implicitly refers to the mass murder of Jews in many places and times, and the notorious part played by some Jewish women in history:

> You shall find them the most eager of men for life. (2:96)

> You see many of them lying in sin and enmity, and how they consume the unlawful; evil is the thing they have been doing. (5:62)

> They hasten about Earth to do corruption there; God loves not the workers of corruption. (5:64)

> We decreed for the Children of Israel in the Book: You shall do corruption on Earth twice. (17:4)

> Do not make mischief on Earth, doing corruption. (2:60)

These verses express the two general disastrous Jewish intrigues against humanity's social life. The Jews have used compound usury, which has shaken human social life. Pitting labor against capital, they have driven the poor to struggle against the rich and have caused the building of banks and the accumulation of wealth through unlawful ways. Also, they usually have been the same nation who, to revenge themselves upon states or governments who have wronged or defeated them, have entered seditionist committees or participated in revolutions.

• From *Surat al-Jumu'a*:

> You of Jewry, if you assert that you are the friends of God, apart from other men, then long for death if you speak truly. But they will never long for it... (62:6-7)

Revealed to refute an assertion of Madina's Jewish community, these verses state that Jews, renowned for their love of life and fear of death, will not give up these traits until the Last Day. *Humiliation and misery were stamped on them* (2:61) states their general fate. Due to such general and awful aspects of their nature and fate, the

Qur'an deals with them severely and criticizes them harshly. Compare with these other aspects of the Qur'anic account of Moses and the Children of Israel. Notice the many gleams of miraculousness behind the Qur'an's simple words and particular topics, like the gleam of miraculous conciseness described in this beam.

*FIFTH BEAM:* This relates to the Qur'an's extraordinarily comprehensive aim, subject matter, meaning, style, beauty, and subtlety. When studied attentively, its *sura*s and verses, particularly the former's opening sections and the latter's beginnings and ends, clearly show that it contains no trace of confusion. And this despite the fact that it contains all types of eloquence, all varieties of fine speech, all categories of elevated style, all examples of good morals and virtues, all principles of natural science, all indexes of knowledge of God, all beneficial rules of individual and social life, and all enlightening laws of creation's exalted reasons and purposes.

Indeed, such a perfect and comprehensive work only can be the work of all-powerful one who sets everything in a miraculous order. It only can be the extraordinary work of a source of miracles like the Qur'an, which sees and shows the truth, is famil-

iar with the Unseen, and bestows guidance. Only
the penetrating expressions of such a work can
rend the veil of the commonplace over things and
events, which causes the compound ignorance leading to unbelief (e.g., atheism and materialism),
and shows the extraordinariness behind that veil.
Only its diamond-like sword of proof can destroy
naturalism (the source of misguidance), remove
thick layers of heedlessness with its thunder-like
cries, and uncover existence's hidden meanings and
creation's mysteries, which are beyond the abilities of all philosophers and scientists.

Unlike other books, the Qur'an does not pursue a series of arguments gradually unfolded on
certain interrelated subjects. Rather, its verses give
the impression that each verse or each group of
verses was sent separately at one time as the codes
of a very solemn and important communication.
Who, other than the universe's Creator, can carry on a communication so concerned with the universe and its Creator as the Qur'an? Who can make
the Majestic Creator speak and cause the universe
to "speak" so truly? In fact, the universe's Owner
speaks and makes the universe speak most serious-

ly and truthfully, and in the most elevated style, in the Qur'an.

No one can find any signs of imitation in it, for there are none. Supposing the impossible, that someone like Musaylima the Liar appeared and managed to make the All-Mighty, All-Compelling, and Majestic Creator of the universe speak as he wishes and make the universe speak to Him, there would be countless signs of imitation and pretence. Every manner of those who put on great airs, even in their basest states, shows their pretence. Consider the following verses, which declare this with an oath: *By the star when it plunged, your comrade is not astray, neither errs, nor speaks out of caprice. This is naught but a Revelation revealed* (53:1-4).

## Third ray

This relates to the Qur'an's miraculous prediction, as well as its freshness and ability to address all levels of understanding regardless of time and place. This ray consists of three radiances.

**FIRST RADIANCE:** This relates to the Qur'an's predictions and has three light-giving aspects.

*FIRST ASPECT:* The Qur'an gives news of the past. Although communicated by an unlettered one, the wise Qur'an mentions in a solemn and powerful manner the important experiences of all Prophets from the time of Adam to the Era of Happiness as well as the main aspects of their mission. The information it provides usually coincides with the commonly agreed descriptions of the previous Scriptures. It also corrects the points on which their corrupted forms disagree. Thus the Qur'an has an all-seeing vision that knows the past better than the previous Scriptures.

Its account of the past is not something rational, but it may be traditional. Tradition is usually particular to lettered persons, whereas the Prophet was unlettered.[31] While the stories of previous Prophets are mentioned mainly in Makkan *sura*s, no one in Makka knew about them. Furthermore, traditions are based partly on hearsay and usually are mixtures of truth and untruth. But the Qur'an speaks of past events as if seeing them.

It extracts the kernel of a long series of events and presents its argument through that kernel. The extracts, summaries, and indications found therein therefore show that the One Who presents them

---

[31] In addition, no local people could tell him about the past. (Tr.)

sees all dimensions of the past. Just as a substantial summary, a fine extract, or a telling example shows a specialist's skill or expert knowledge, the Qur'an's chief points and main themes, chosen from certain events, show that the One Who chooses them has an all-encompassing knowledge of the whole and is describing them with an extraordinary skill.

*SECOND ASPECT:* This relates to the Qur'an's many categories of predictions, one being particular to saints and spiritual unveiling. For instance, Muhiy al-Din ibn al-'Arabi found many predictions in *Surat al-Rum*. Imam Rabbani discovered signs of many future events in the *muqatta'at* (the individual, disjunct letters at the beginning of certain *sura*s). For scholars of its inner aspects and esoteric meanings and of creation, the Qur'an is full of predictions. I will focus on only one and be content with giving some examples, without going into detail.

The Qur'an says to the Messenger:

> So be patient: Surely God's promise is true. (30:60)

> You shall enter the Holy Mosque, if God wills, in security, your heads shaved, your hair cut short, not fearing. (48:27)

It is He who has sent His Messenger with the guidance and the religion of truth, that He may uplift it above every religion. (48:28)

The Romans have been vanquished in the nearer part of the land; and, after their vanquishing, they shall be the victors in a few years. To God belongs the Command. (30:3-4)

You shall see, and they will see, which of you is demented. (68: 5-6)

Or do they say: "He is a poet for whom we await what fate will bring." Say: "Wait. I shall be waiting with you." (52:30-31)

God will protect you from people. (5:67)

If you are in doubt concerning what We have sent down on Our servant, bring a sura like it and call your witnesses, helpers, apart from God, if you are truthful. If you do not—and you will never do it— then fear the fire... (2:23-24)

Say: "If the Last Abode with God is yours exclusively, and not for other people, then long for death— if you speak truly." But they will never long for it. (2:94)

We shall show them Our signs in the outer world and in themselves till it is clear to them that it is the truth. (41:53)

Say: "If humanity and jinn banded together to produce the like of this Qur'an, they would never produce its like, even though they backed one another." (17:88)

God will bring a people He loves and who love Him, humble toward believers, mighty and dignified against unbelievers, (people) who struggle in the way of God, not fearing the reproach of any reproacher. (5:54)

Say: "All praise be to God. He shall show you His signs and you will recognize them." (27:93)

Say: "He is the All-Merciful. We believe in Him and in Him we put all our trust. Assuredly, you will soon know who is in manifest error." (67:29)

God has promised those of you who believe and do righteous deeds that He will make you successors in the land, even as He made those who were before them successors, and that He will establish their religion for them, that He has approved for them, and will bring them into security after their fear. (24:55)

All of the predictions made in these verses came true. So if a person who was subject to the severest criticisms and objections, in whom even one fault was certain to lead to his cause's failure, makes predictions so unhesitatingly and confidently, and in such a serious manner, it shows without doubt that he speaks not of himself but of what he receives from his Eternal Teacher.

*THIRD ASPECT:* This relates to what the Qur'an says about the Unseen, Divine truths, and the Hereafter's realities. Certain truths of creation also may be considered in this category.

The Qur'an's explanations in these areas are among the most important pieces of information about the Unseen. Humanity cannot advance in a straight direction amid paths of misguidance and reach the Unseen's truths or realities. The deep, endless disagreements between schools of philosophy and scientists show that even their greatest geniuses cannot discover even the least of these truths by unaided reasoning. With purified souls, refined hearts, evolved spirits, and intellects perfected by the Qur'an, humanity could perceive and accept those truths and realities, and then could say only: "May God bless the Qur'an."

No one can discover and perceive the Hereafter's events, states, conditions, and stages, including the life of the grave, by himself or herself. However, one can penetrate and comprehend them via the Qur'an's light, as if seeing and observing them clearly. You may refer to The Tenth Word, which discusses how right and true are the Qur'an's explanations of that Unseen world of the Hereafter.

**SECOND RADIANCE:** This relates to the Qur'an's freshness, which is maintained as if it were revealed anew in every era. As an eternal discourse addressing all humanity regardless of time or place and level of understanding, it should—and does—have a never-fading freshness.

The Qur'an so impresses each new generation that each one regards it as being revealed to itself and receives its instructions therefrom. Human words and laws become old and so need to be revised or changed. But the Qur'an's laws and principles are so established and constant, so compatible with essential human nature and creation's unchanging laws, that the passage of time has no effect upon them. Instead, it shows the Qur'an's truth, validity, and force even more clearly!

This twentieth century, including its People of the Book,[32] is more confident of itself than preceding ones, and yet most in need of the Qur'anic wisdom beginning with: *O People of the Book.* As this

---

[32] Jews and Christians.

phrase also means "O people of schooling and education," those messages seem to be directed toward this century exclusively. With all its strength and freshness, the Qur'an calls to us:

> Say: "O People of the Book, come now to a word common between us and you, that we serve none but God, and that we associate not anything with Him, and do not some of us take others as lords, apart from God." (3:64)

Our present civilization, the product of human ideas and perhaps of the jinn, has chosen to argue with the Qur'an. It tries to contradict its miraculousness through its charm and "spells." To prove the Qur'an's miraculousness against this new, terrible opponent, and affirm its challenge of:

> Say: "If humanity and jinn banded together to produce the like of this Qur'an, they would never produce its like, not though they backed one another" (17:88),

I will compare modern civilization's principles and foundations with those of the Qur'an.

First, all of the comparisons and criteria put forward so far, and the truths and verses contained therein, prove the Qur'an's miraculousness and indisputable superiority over modern civilization.

Second, as convincingly argued in The Twelfth Word: Modern civilization says that the point of support in social life is force or power, the aim of life is to realize self-interest, conflict is the principle of relationship in life, the bond between communities is racism and negative nationalism, and its fruits are the gratification of carnal desires and the multiplication of human needs.

In addition, force calls for aggression, and gratification of self-interest causes conflict over material resources. Conflict brings strife. Racism feeds itself by swallowing others, and so paves the way for aggression. Thus despite modern civilization's advantages and positive aspects, only 20 percent of people are superficially contented while the other 80 percent are in hardship and misery.

In contrast, the Qur'an accepts right as the point of support in social life, considers the aim of life to be virtue and God's approval, recognizes mutual assistance as the principle of relationship in life, and accepts ties of religion, profession, and citizenship as the bonds between communities. It seeks to place a barrier against the illicit attacks of lust, urges the soul to ennoble and satisfy its lofty aspirations, and encourages people to perfection and so makes them truly human.

Right calls for unity; virtue brings mutual support and solidarity. Mutual assistance means helping each other. Religion secures brotherhood (and sisterhood) and mutual attraction, while restraining the carnal self and urging the soul to perfection bring happiness in this world and the next.

Thus despite its borrowings from previous Divine religions and especially the Qur'an, which accounts for its agreeable aspects, modern civilization cannot offer a viable alternative to the Qur'an.

Third, I will give a few examples of the Qur'an's many subjects and commandments. As its laws and principles transcend time and space, they do not become obsolete. For example, despite all its charitable foundations, institutions of intellectual and moral training, and severe disciplines and laws and regulations, modern civilization has been defeated by the Qur'an in the following matters:

*FIRST COMPARISON:* Perform the prescribed prayer, and pay the *zakat* (2:43) and: God has made trading lawful and usury unlawful (2:275). As explained in my *Isharat al-I'jaz*, the following two attitudes or approaches are the causes of all revolutions and social upheavals, as well as the root of all moral failings. They can be summed up, respectively, as: "I do not care if others die of hunger so long as my stomach is full," and: "You must bear the costs of my ease—you must work so that I may eat."

A peaceful social life depends on the balance between the elite (rich) and common (poor) people.[33] This balance is based on the former's care and compassion and the latter's respect and obedience. Ignoring the first attitude drives the rich to wrongdoing, usurpation, immorality, and mercilessness; ignoring the second attitude drives the poor to hatred, grudges, envy, and conflict with the rich. This conflict has destroyed social peace for the

---

[33] Said Nursi uses *elite* for those who can give *zakat*, and the *masses* for those eligible to receive it. These designations are relative, for they depend upon the local standard of richness. As Islam does not allow a deep socioeconomic gap to form between Muslims, the gap between these groups is not very great. In many Muslim societies today, members of both groups can be found within the middle class. As the main purpose for *zakat* is for the poor to receive enough money to provide for their families, we should consider the living standard envisaged by Islam when considering *zakat*. (Tr.)

last 2 or 3 centuries, especially in Europe's social upheavals, all of which are rooted in the century-old struggle between labor and capital.

Despite all its charitable societies, institutions of moral training, and severe laws and regulations, modern civilization has neither reconciled these two social classes nor healed those two severe wounds of human life. The Qur'an, however, eradicates the first attitude and heals its wounds through *zakat*, and eradicates the second by outlawing interest. The Qur'an stands at the door of the world and turns away interest. It says to us: "If you want to end social conflict and struggle, do not engage in interest," and orders its students to avoid such things.

*SECOND COMPARISON:* Modern civilization rejects polygamy as unwise and disadvantageous to social life, even though if the purpose of marriage were sexual gratification, polygamy would be a lawful way to realize it. The Qur'an permits a man to have more than one wife under certain circumstances. However, as observed even in animals and plants, the purpose for and wisdom in sexual relations is reproduction. The resulting pleasure is a small payment determined by Divine Mercy to realize this duty.

Marriage is for reproduction and perpetuation of the species. Being able to give birth at most once a year, to become pregnant during half of a month, and entering menopause around 50, one woman is usually insufficient for a man, who can sometimes impregnate even until the age of 100. That is why, in most cases, modern civilization tolerates prostitution.

*THIRD COMPARISON:* Modern civilization criticizes the Qur'an for giving a woman one-third of the inheritance (half of her brother's share) while giving a man two-thirds. However, general circumstances are considered when establishing general rules and laws. In this case, a woman usually finds a man to maintain her, whereas a man usually has to take care of someone else.[34] Given this, a woman's

---

[34] According to the Qur'an, the husband is legally responsible for providing for the family. However rich, the wife has no legal obligation to contribute to the family's livelihood. Second, as the wife is free to multiply her wealth through such undertakings as trade, the Qur'an does not force her to be economically dependent upon her husband. Therefore the Qur'an's distribution of inheritance has psychological, social, and economic motives and implications. For more information, consult The Eleventh Letter of Said Nursi, *The Letters* (Turkey: The Light, Inc., 2002). (Tr.)

husband is to make up the difference between her share of the inheritance and that of her brother. Her brother, on the other hand, will spend half of his inheritance on his wife, equaling his sister's share. This is true justice.

*FOURTH COMPARISON:* The Qur'an prohibits idolatry and condemns the worship of images, which can be an imitation of idolatry. However, modern civilization sees sculpture and the portrayal of living beings, which the Qur'an condemns, as one of its virtues. Forms with or without shadows (sculptures and pictures of living beings) are either a petrified tyranny (tyranny represented in stone), embodied ostentation or caprice, all of which urge people to tyranny, ostentation, and capriciousness.

Out of compassion, the Qur'an orders women to wear the veil of modesty to maintain respect for them and to prevent their transformation into objects of low desire or being used to excite lust. Modern civilization has drawn women out of their homes, torn aside their veils, and led humanity into corruption. Family life is based on mutual love and respect between modest men and women; modern civilization has destroyed sincere love and respect, and poisoned family life.

Sculptures and pictures, especially obscene ones, have a great share in this moral corruption and spiritual degeneration. Just as looking at the corpse of a beautiful woman who deserves compassion with lust and desire destroys morality, looking lustfully at pictures of living women, which are like little corpses, troubles and diverts, shakes and destroys elevated human feelings.

In conclusion, then, besides securing happiness for all people in this world, the Qur'anic commandments serve their eternal happiness. Compare other subjects with those mentioned.

Modern civilization stands defeated before the Qur'an's rules and principles for social life and humanity, and bankrupt before the Qur'an's miraculous content. The Words written so far, primarily the Eleventh and Twelfth, demonstrate that European philosophy and scientism, the spirit of that civilization, are helpless when confronted with the Qur'an's wisdom. In addition, when compared to its literary merits—which may be likened to an elevated lover's uplifting songs arising from temporary separation or heroic epics encouraging its audience to victory and lofty sacrifices—modern civilization's literature and rhetoric appear as an orphan's desperate, grief-stricken wailing or a drunkard's noise.

Styles of literature and rhetoric give rise to sorrow or joy. Sorrow is of two kinds: loneliness and lack of any protection and support, or separation from the beloved. The first is despairing and produced by modern misguided naturalist, and heedless civilization. The second is lofty and exhilarating, and arouses a hope and eagerness for reunion. This is the kind given by the guiding, light-diffusing Qur'an.

Joy also is of two kinds. The first incites the soul to animal desires (so-called "fine" arts, drama, and cinema, etc.). The second restrains the carnal self and urges (in a mannerly, innocent way) the human heart, spirit, intellect, and all inner senses and faculties to lofty things and reunion with the original, eternal abode and with friends who have passed on already. The Qur'an encourages this joy by arousing an eagerness to reach Paradise, eternal happiness, and the vision of God.

Thus the profound meaning and great truth contained in:

> Say: "If humanity and jinn banded together to produce the like of this Qur'an, they would never pro-

duce its like, even if they backed one another"
(17:88),

is not, as some assert, an exaggeration. It is pure truth and reality, which the long history of Islam has proved.

The challenge contained here has two principal aspects. One is that no human or jinn work can resemble or equal the Qur'an's style, eloquence, rhetoric, wording, comprehensiveness, conciseness, and profundity. Nor can their most beautiful and eloquent words, all arranged in a volume by their most competent representatives, equal the Qur'an. The second aspect is that all human and jinn civilizations, philosophies, literatures, and laws, regardless of apparent profundity and beauty, are dim and helpless when faced with the Qur'an's commandments, wisdom, and eloquence.

*THIRD RADIANCE:* The wise Qur'an informs all people, regardless of time, place, or level of understanding, of God, Islam, and belief. There-fore it has to teach each group and level in an appropriate manner. As people are very diverse, the Qur'an must contain enough levels for all of them. I will illustrate this briefly by pointing out a few minor points.

- From *Surat al-Ikhlas*:

  > He begets not, nor was begotten. And there is none comparable to Him. (112:3-4)

Ordinary people, the majority of humanity, understand that Almighty God has no parents, children, wives, and equals. Those having relatively higher levels of understanding will infer that the verses reject Jesus' supposed (by Christians) Divine sonship and divinity, and the divinity of angels and all beings who beget and are begotten.

Now, since rejecting a negation or an impossibility is useless, according to the science of eloquence, it must have another important, useful import. As God does not beget and was not begotten, this rejection must serve another purpose: Whoever has parents, children, and equals cannot be God and so does not deserve worship. This is one reason why *Surat al-Ikhlas*, from which the above verses are quoted, is of such great use for all persons at all times.

Those with a higher degree of understanding derive the meaning that Almighty God is free of all relationships with the creation that suggest begetting and being begotten, and that He has no partners, helpers, or fellow deities. He is the Creator, and everything and everyone else is the created. God creates with the command *"Be! and it is"* and through His eternal Will. He is abso-lutely free of every quality suggesting compulsion or obligation, and unwilled, unintended action, for these would be contrary to His absolute perfection.

Another group with an even higher level of understanding infers that Almighty God is eternal, without beginning or end, and is the First and the Last. He has no equals, peers, likes, or anything similar or analogous to Him in His Being, Attributes, or acts. However, to make His acts understandable, the Qur'an allows recourse to proper comparisons. You may compare to these understandings the views of those with perfect knowledge and love of God, and most truthful, painstaking scholars.

• From *Surat al-Ahzab*:

> Muhammad is not the father of any of your men. (33:40)

Ordinary people understand that Zayd, the servant of God's Messenger and his adopted son, divorced his wife Zaynab because he found her superior to him in virtue. By God's command, God's Messenger then married her. Therefore the verse says: "If the Prophet calls you 'son,' this is because of his mission as Messenger. Biologically, he is not the father of any of your men, which would prevent him from marrying one of your widows."

A second group derives this meaning: "A superior treats his subjects with fatherly care and compassion. If that superior is both a worldly ruler and a spiritual guide, his compassion will be far greater than a father's. His subjects consider him a real father."

Since this may cause people to have difficulty in seeing the Prophet, whom they consider more fatherly than a father, as the husband of their women, the Qur'an corrects this view: "The Prophet considers you with the view of Divine compassion and treats you as a father. You are like his children from the viewpoint of his mission. But he is not your biological father, which would make it improper for him to marry one of your women."

A third group understands that merely because of their connection with the Prophet, as well as their reliance on his perfections and fatherly compassion, believers cannot believe that their salvation is assured even though they commit sins and errors.[35]

A fourth group deduces a prediction: The Prophet will not have a son to continue his line. His sons will die young. As expressed by *men*, that is, as he will not be the father of *men*, he will be the father of daughters. Thus his line will continue through his daughter.

> All praise be to God, the blessed children of his daughter Fatima, his two grandsons Hasan and Husayn, the "light-giving moons" of the two illustrious lines, continue the line of the Sun of Prophethood both biologically and spiritually. O God, bestow blessings on him and his Family.

## Second light

This second light has three rays.

### First ray

The Qur'an is a book of perfect fluency, superb clarity and soundness, firm coherence, and well-

---

[35] For example, some Alawis do not perform the prescribed prayers and say that their prayers have been performed already. Christians delude themselves that Jesus sacrificed himself for their salvation, and so rely on their leader's or guide's perfections and are lazy when it comes to observing religious commandments.)

established harmony and proportion. There is a strong, mutual support and interrelation among its sentences and their parts, and an elevated correspondence among its verses and their purposes. Such leading figures in Arabic philology, literature, and semantics as al-Zamakhshari, al-Sakkaki, and 'Abd al-Qahir al-Jurjani testify to this.

In addition, although seven or eight factors counter fluency, soundness, coherence, harmony, proportion, interrelation, and correspondence, these factors rather enrich the Qur'an's fluency, soundness, and coherence. Like branches and twigs stemming from a fruit-producing tree's trunk and completing the tree's beauty and growth, these factors sometimes do not cause discord in the fluent harmony of the Qur'an's composition, but rather express new, richer, and complementary meanings.

Consider the following facts:

- Although the Qur'an was revealed in parts over 23 years for different needs and purposes, it has such a perfect harmony that it is as if it were revealed all at once.

- Although the Qur'an was revealed over 23 years on different occasions, its parts are so mutually supportive that it is as if it were revealed all at once.

- Although the Qur'an came in answer to different and repeated questions, its parts are so united and harmonious with each other that it is as if it were the answer to a single question.

- Although the Qur'an came to judge diverse cases and events, it displays such a perfect order that it is as if it were the judgment delivered on a single case or event.

- Although the Qur'an was revealed by Divine courtesy in styles varied to suit innumerable people of different levels of understanding, moods, and temperament, its parts exhibit so beautiful a similarity, correspondence, and fluency that it is as if it were addressing one degree of understanding and temperament.

- Although the Qur'an speaks to countless varieties of people who are remote from each one in time, space, and character, it has such an easy way of explanation, pure style, and clear way of description that it is as if it were addressing one homogenous group, with each different

group thinking that it is being addressed unique-
ly and specifically.

• Although the Qur'an was revealed for the gradual guidance of different peoples with various
purposes, it has such a perfect straightforward-
ness, sensitive balance, and beautiful order that
it is as if it were pursuing only one purpose.

Despite being the reasons of confusion, these
factors add to the miraculousness of the Qur'an's
explanations and to its fluency of style and harmony. Anyone with an undiseased heart, a sound
conscience, and good taste sees graceful fluency,
exquisite proportion, pleasant harmony, and matchless eloquence in its explanations. Anyone with a
sound power of sight and insight sees that the
Qur'an has an eye with which to see the whole universe, with all its inner and outer dimensions, like
a single page and to read all the meanings contained in it. Since I would need many volumes to
explain this truth with examples, please refer to
my *Isharat al-I'jaz* and *the Words* written so far.

### Second ray

This relates to the Qur'an's miraculous qualities displayed by means of its summaries and

unique style of using God's Beautiful Names to end many of its verses.

> NOTE: This ray contains many verses that serve as examples for this ray and for other previously discussed matters. So I mention them briefly.

The Qur'an generally ends its verses with summaries that comprise those Divine Beautiful Names in which the contents of the verses originate, contain in a summarized form all meanings of the verses or all-comprehensive principles concerning the Qur'an's main aims, confirm and corroborate the verses, or incite the mind to meditation. Given this, these summaries contain traces from the Qur'an's elevated wisdom, drops from the water of life of Divine guidance, or sparks from the lightning of the Qur'an's miraculousness.

I will discuss briefly only 10 of the numerous traces, and mention only one of the many examples of each trace's several aspects. I will append a brief statement of the meaning of one of the many truths contained in each example. Most traces are found together in most of the verses and form a real design of miraculousness. Most of the verses given as examples are also examples for most of the traces. With respect to verses mentioned in previous Words, I will make a short reference to the meanings of those cited here.

**FIRST QUALITY OF ELOQUENCE:** With its miraculous expression, the Qur'an spreads out the Majestic Maker's acts and works. It then concludes either with the Divine Name or Names originating those acts and works, as with proof of an essential aim of the Qur'an (e.g., Divine Unity or Resurrection).

For example, in: *He created for you all that is in Earth. Then He turned to the heaven, and fashioned it as seven heavens. He is the Knower of all things* (2:29), the verse relates, in a manner leading to a particular result or important goal, the most comprehensive works, all of which testify to Divine Knowledge and Power via their purposes and order, and concludes with the Name "the Knower."

In: *Have We not made Earth a cradle, and the mountains masts? And We have created you in pairs ... Surely the Day of Decision is a time appointed* (78:6-8, 17), it mentions Almighty God's mighty acts and tremendous works and concludes with the Day of Resurrection (the Day of Judgment).

**SECOND POINT OF ELOQUENCE:** The Qur'an lays out the works of Divine art without specifying the Divine Name originating each work, and concludes by either mentioning the Names together or referring them to the intellect. For example:

> Say: "Who provides for you from the sky and Earth, or who owns all hearing and sight (of which you have a portion); and who brings forth the living from the dead and the dead from the living; who rules and directs all affairs?" They will say: "God." Then say: "Will you not then fear (God) and keep your duty (concerning both this world and the next)? Such then is God, your Lord, the Truth." (10:31-32)

At the beginning, it asks: "Who, having prepared the heaven and Earth as two sources of your provision, sends rain from there and brings forth grains from here? Who but He subjugates the heaven and Earth as two stores of your provision? That being so, praise and thanksgiving are due to Him exclusively." In the second part it means: "Who owns your eyes and ears, which are your most precious bodily parts? From which shop or factory did you buy them? Only your Lord can give you these subtle faculties of hearing and sight. He also creates and nurtures you. Therefore, there is no Lord but He, and only He deserves worship."

In the third part, it signifies: "Who gives life to the dead Earth every spring, and quickens innumerable species that died in the previous autumn or winter? Who but the Truth, the Creator of the whole universe, can do that? As He gives life to Earth, He will also resurrect you and send you to a Supreme Tribunal."

In the fourth part it explains: "Who but God can administer this vast universe with perfect order? Since only He can do that, the Power easily governing the universe and its various spheres is so perfect and infinite that It needs no partners and helpers. The One Who governs the universe does not leave smaller creatures to other hands. Therefore you must admit God willingly or unwillingly."

The first and fourth parts suggest God, while the second suggests the Lord and the third suggests the Truth. Understand from this the miraculousness of *Such then is God, your Lord, the Truth*. After presenting the mighty acts of Almighty God, and the important products of His Power, the Qur'an mentions the Names God, the Lord and the

Truth, and thereby points out the origin of those acts and products.

An example of how the Qur'an urges the human intellect to reflect on His works and recognize Him is presented below:

> In the creation of the heavens and Earth, the alternation of night and day, the ships sailing on the sea for humanity's benefit, the water which God sends down from the sky and thereby reviving Earth after its death, and dispersing all kinds of beasts therein, (in His) directing and disposal of the winds, and the clouds subjugated between heaven and Earth, are signs for people who use their intellects. (2:164)

The verse enumerates the works and manifestations of Divine creation, such as showing Divine Sovereignty by creating the heavens and Earth; of Divine Lordship in alternating night and day, demonstrating the perfection of Almighty God's Power and the grandeur of His Lordship, and testifying to His Oneness; showing Mercy by subduing the sea and the ship, which are of great use for human social life; manifesting Power's greatness in sending rain to revive Earth and its innumerable creatures, and to make it like an exquisite place of resurrection and gathering; manifesting

Power and Compassion in creating innumerable animals from soil; manifesting Mercy and Wisdom in charging the winds to pollinate plants and to allow animate beings to breathe; manifesting Lordship in accumulating and dispersing the clouds (means of Mercy), and suspending them between the heavens and Earth.

After enumerating such works and manifestations of Divine acting without mentioning the Names originating them, the verse concludes ... *are signs for people who use their intellects* and urges the intellect to reflect fully on the truths they contain.

**THIRD QUALITY OF ELOQUENCE:** Sometimes the Qur'an describes Almighty God's acts in detail and concludes with a summary. It uses detailed description to give conviction, and then impresses them on the mind by summarizing them.

• From *Sura Yusuf*:

> So will your Lord choose you, and teach you the interpretation of dreams, and all social and natural phenomena, and perfect His blessing upon you and upon the family of Jacob, as He perfected it formerly on your forefathers Abraham and Isaac. Your Lord is All-Knowing, All-Wise. (12:6)

This verse points to the Divine blessings on Prophet Joseph, his father and forefathers, and says: "He has distinguished you (Joseph) with Prophethood and, by connecting the chain of Prophets to yours, made your lineage the most honored and prominent. He has made your house a place of education and guidance in which knowledge of God and Divine wisdom are taught, and combined in you, by means of that knowledge and wisdom, felicitous spiritual sovereignty of the world with eternal happiness in the Hereafter. He will equip you with that knowledge and wisdom and make you a dignified ruler, a noble Prophet, and a wise guide."

By concluding with *Your Lord is All-Knowing, All-Wise*, the verse summarizes all those blessings and means: "Your Lord is the All-Knowing and All-Wise. His Lordship and Wisdom require that He shall manifest His Names the All-Knowing and the All-Wise through you and make you a knowledgeable and wise one, as He did your father and forefathers."

• From *Surat Al-'Imran:*

> Say: "O God, Master of the Kingdom, You give the Kingdom to whom You will, and seize the Kingdom

> from whom You will. You exalt whom You will and You abase whom You will. In Your hand is the good. You are Powerful over everything. You make the night enter into the day and the day enter into the night. You bring forth the living from the dead and the dead from the living. You provide whoever You will without measure." (3:26-27)

These verses point out God's execution of His Laws in humanity's social life and the universe. They emphasize that honor and degradation, as well as wealth and poverty, depend directly on Almighty God's Will and Choice. Nothing, not even the most insignificant happenings in the Realm of Multiplicity, is beyond the domain of Divine Will, and so there is no place for chance.

After pointing out this essential principle, the verse affirms that our provision, which is most essential in this worldly life, originates directly from the Real Provider's treasury of Mercy, and means: "Your provision depends on Earth's vitality, the revival of which is possible through the coming of spring. Only the One Who has subdued the sun and the moon, and alternates night and day, can bring spring. If this is so, then only the One Who fills Earth's surface with fruits can provide someone with an apple and become one's real provider."

By concluding with *and You provide whomever You will without measure,* the verses summarize all acts previously described in detail and affirm that the One Who provides you without measure does all those things.

**FOURTH POINT OF ELOQUENCE:** Sometimes the Qur'an mentions God's creation and creatures in a certain series. By showing that their existence and life have a purposeful order and balance, it seems to give them a certain radiance and brightness. Then it points to the Divine Name or Names originating that order, which, like mirrors, reflect Him. It is as if each mentioned creature were a word and the Names were those words' meanings, or each creature were a fruit and the Names were their seeds or substantial parts. For example:

- From *Surat al-Mu'minun:*

> We created humanity of an extraction of clay. Then We set a sperm in a safe lodging, and then created the sperm drop into something suspended (on the womb's wall). We created that suspended thing into something like a lump of chewed flesh, and created bones from that lump, and clothed the bones in

muscular tissue. Then We built humanity in another creation. So blessed be God, of the highest and most blessed degree of creating. (23:12-14)

The Qur'an mentions the extraordinary and wonderful, well-ordered, well-proportioned stages of humanity's creation in such a manner that, as if in a mirror, *So blessed be God, of the highest and most blessed degree of creating* is seen in it, with the result that whoever reads or listens to it cannot help saying that same phrase of blessing. A scribe used by God's Messenger to record the Revela-tions uttered this phrase before the Messenger recited it, so that the scribe wondered whether he too was receiving Revelation. But in reality, it was the verses' perfect order, coherence, and clarity that led to that phrase even before its recitation.

• From *Surat al-A'raf:*

> Your Lord is God, Who created the heavens and Earth in 6 days—then set Himself upon the Supreme Throne, covering the day with the night, pursuing each other urgently—and the sun, the moon, and the stars subservient, by His command. Truly, His are the creation and the command. Blessed be God, the Lord of the worlds. (7:54)

Here the Qur'an shows the tremendousness of God's Power and His Lordship's sovereignty by indicating how the sun, moon, and stars obey His commands; and the Majesty of the All-Powerful One seated on the Throne of Lordship, Who, by making night and day continuously follow each other like white and black ribbons or lines, writes His Lordship's sign on the universe's pages.

Therefore, whoever reads or hears this verse feels eagerness to utter *Blessed be God, the Lord of the worlds.* Thus this phrase summarizes the preceding lines in the context, its substance or seed or fruit.

**FIFTH QUALITY OF ELOQUENCE:** The Qur'an sometimes mentions certain physical or material things or substances of various qualities and subject to change and disintegration. Then, in order to transform them into stable and unchanging realities, it connects and concludes them with certain universal and permanent Divine Names, or concludes with a summary urging reflection and taking a lesson.

• From *Surat al-Baqara:*

> He taught Adam all of the names; then He present-
> ed them unto the angels and said: "Now tell me the

> names of these, if you speak truly." They said: "Glory
> be to You, we have no knowledge save only what
> You have taught us. You are the All-Knowing, All-
> Wise." (2:31-32)

The verses first mention that Adam is superior to angels in being God's vicegerent due to the knowledge he received as a Divine gift, and then the angels' defeat before Adam with regard to knowledge. The Qur'an concludes its description of this event with two universal Names: *the All-Knowing, All-Wise.* Thus the angels acknowledge: "Since You are the All-Knowing and All-Wise, You instructed Adam in the Names and made him superior to us through that knowledge. You are the All-Wise, and therefore give us according to our capacities and give him superiority because of his capacity."

• From *Surat al-Nahl:*

> There is a lesson for you in cattle. We give you to
> drink of what is in their bellies, between filth and
> blood, pure milk, sweet to drinkers. You take from
> the fruits of the palms and vines a strong drink and
> a fair provision. In that is a sign for a people who
> understand. Your Lord inspired the bee, saying: "Take
> for yourself, of mountains, houses, and trees, and
> of what they are building. Then eat of every kind

of fruit and follow the ways of your Lord, easy to go upon." Then comes out of their bellies a fluid of diverse hues wherein is healing for people. In this is a sign for a people who reflect. (16:66-69)

After showing that Almighty God has made some animals (e.g., sheep, goats, cows, and camels) sources of pure and delicious milk; some of His plant creatures (e.g., date palms and vines) tables of sweet, pleasant, delicious bounties; and some of His Power's miracles (e.g., the bee, a producer of honey that contains healing) to urge humanity to compare similar gifts with these and so reflect and take lessons, the verses conclude with *In this is a sign for a people who reflect.*

**SIXTH POINT OF ELOQUENCE:** Sometimes a verse lays out many results and decrees of Divine Lordship and unites them with a bond of unity or inserts a universal principle.

• From *Surat al-Baqara:*

> God, there is no god but He, the Living, the Self-Subsistent. Slumber overtakes Him not, nor sleep. To Him belongs all that is in the heavens and what is in Earth. Who is there that shall intercede with Him save with His permission? He knows what is before them (in time and space) and what is behind

them (in time and space), and they comprehend nothing of His Knowledge save such as He wills. His
Seat comprises the heavens and Earth, and upholding them does not oppress Him. He is the All-High,
the Tremendous. (2:255)

Together with proving Divine Unity in 10 ways,
this verse, called the Verse of the (Supreme) Throne,
rejects and refutes associating partners with God
with the question: *Who is there that shall inter-
cede with Him save with His permission?* Further,
since God's Greatest Name is manifested here,
the meanings it contains concerning Divine truths
are of the highest degree.

It also shows an act expressive of Lordship in
Its highest degree. Moreover, after mentioning
God's all-encompassing preserving or upholding
in the greatest degree—His simultaneous control
of the heavens and Earth—as a bond of unity or
an aspect of oneness, it summarizes their origins
in *He is the All-High, the Tremendous.*

• From *Surat Ibrahim:*

God created the heavens and Earth and sends down
from heaven water wherewith He brings forth fruits
for your sustenance. He subjected to you the ships
to run upon the sea at His command; He subjected

to you the sun and moon constant upon their courses, and He subjected to you the night and day and
gives you of all that you ask Him. If you count the
bounties of God, you can never number them.
(14:32-34)

These verses show how Almighty God created this universe like a palace and how, making
the heavens and Earth like two servants for us,
He sends rain to provide for us. They also state
that He has subjected ships to us so that all may
benefit from fruits and grains grown elsewhere
and may make their livelihood through bartering
their produce. In other words, He created the sea,
the winds, and trees in such a way and with such
qualities that the wind serves as a whip, the ship
as a horse, and the sea as a desert.

In addition to enabling us to have global relations through ships, He made mighty rivers a natural means of transportation. To bring about seasons and present His bounties produced therein
to us, the True Giver of Bounties made the sun
and moon run on their courses and created them
like two obedient servants or wheels to steer that
vast revolving machine. He has appointed the night

as a cloak, a cover for our rest and sleep, and the day as a means for making our livelihood.

After enumerating these favors to show how broad is their circle and how uncountable are the favors in themselves, the verses end in this summary: *He gives you of all that you ask Him. If you count the bounties of God, you can never number them.* In other words, God gives to us whatever we ask for in the tongue of capacity and natural neediness. His favors are beyond counting. If they are presented in terms of the heavens and Earth, as well as the sun and the moon, the night and the day, then of course it is impossible to count them.

**SEVENTH MANIFESTATION OF ELOQUENCE:** To show that apparent causes have no creative part in bringing about the associated effect or result, the Qur'an sometimes presents the purposes for something's existence and the results it yields. This shows that unconscious and lifeless causes are only apparent veils, and that very wise purposes and significant results can be willed and pursued only by an All-Knowing and All-Wise One.

By mentioning the purposes and results, the Qur'an shows the great distance between the cause and result, regardless of what our eyes tell us. No cause, no matter how great, can produce the smallest result. Thus the Divine Names appear as stars and connect them with each other. Like a line of mountain peaks seeming to meet the sky on the horizon, despite the vast space between them in which the stars rise and set, the distance between causes and results is so great that it can only be seen through belief and the Qur'an's light.

• From *Surat 'Abasa:*

> Let people consider the food (they eat): We pour out rain abundantly, then We split Earth in fissures and therein make the grains grow, as well as grapes, fresh herbage, olives, palms, enclosed gardens dense with lofty trees, and fruits and pastures, provision for you and your cattle. (80:24-32)

The verses first mention Divine Power's miracles in a purposeful order together with their apparent causes, and then, through provision for you and your cattle, draw attention to the purpose behind them. They then prove that there is a free Agent pursuing that purpose, along with the series of all those causes and results, and that causes are only a veil hiding Him from manifest sight.

Through the same phrase, the verses declare that material or natural causes have no creative part in bringing about the results and mean: "The water necessary for you and your cattle comes from heaven. Since it cannot have mercy on you and your cattle and thereby provide for you, it does not come by itself; rather, it is sent down. Then Earth splits in clefts for vegetation to grow in and provide you with food. As the unfeeling, unconscious Earth cannot consider your provision or have mercy on you, it does not split by itself; rather, someone opens that 'door' to you and hands you your provision. Since pastures and trees do not think about your provision or producing fruits and grains for you out of mercy, they are only threads, ropes, or cables that an All-Wise, All-Merciful One stretches out from behind a veil to extend His bounties to living beings." Thus several Divine Names like the All-Merciful, All-Compassionate, All-Provider, All-Giver of Bounties, and All-Magnificent manifest themselves in these verses, even though they are not mentioned.

- From *Surat al-Nur:*

> Do you not see how God drives the clouds lightly, then gathers them together in piles and completes

the circuit between them? Then you see rain issuing out of their midst. He causes (clouds like) mountains charged with hail to descend from heaven, and makes it fall on whom He wills, and from whom He wills He turns it aside. The brightness of His lightning all but takes away the sight. God turns about the night and the day. Truly, in that is a lesson for people of insight. God created every moving creature of water. Some of them go on their bellies, some go on two feet, and some go on four feet. God creates whatever He wills. God is All-Powerful over all things. (24:43-45)

These verses explain the curious Divine disposals in sending rain from accumulated clouds, which are among the Divine Lordship's most important miracles and the most curious veils over the Divine treasuries of Mercy. While the cloud's atoms are scattered in the atmosphere, they come together to form a cloud at God's command, just like a dispersed army assembling at the call of a trumpet. Then, like small troops coming from different directions to form an army, God joins the clouds together to enable the completion of an electric circuit between them. He causes those piled-up clouds, charged with rain or snow or hail, to pour down the water of life to all living beings on Earth.

Rain does not fall by itself, but is sent to meet certain purposes and according to need. While the atmosphere is clear and no clouds can be seen, the mountain-like forms of clouds, gathered like a striking assembly, assemble because the One Who knows all living beings and their needs gathers them together to send rain therefrom. These events suggest several Divine Names: the All-Powerful, All-Knowing, All-Disposer of Things, All-Arranger, All-Upbringing, All-Helper, and Reviver.

**EIGHTH QUALITY OF ELOQUENCE:** To convince our hearts of God Almighty's wonderful acts in the Hereafter, and to prepare our intellects to confirm them, the Qur'an sometimes mentions His amazing actions in the world. In other places, it describes His miraculous acts pertaining to the future and the Hereafter in such a manner that we are convinced of them due to something with which we are familiar in our own lives.

• From *Sura Ya Sin:*

> Does humanity not regard how We created it of a sperm-drop? Yet humanity is a manifest adversary. Humanity has coined for Us a similitude and has forgotten its creation. It asks: "Who will revive the bones when they have rotted away?" Say: "He will

revive them Who originated them the first time. He knows all creation, Who has made for you fire out of the green tree and lo, from it you kindle." Is not He Who created the heavens and Earth able to create the like of them? Yes indeed. He is the All-Creator, the All-Knowing. His command, when He wills a thing, is to say to it 'Be,' and it is. So glory be to Him, in Whose hand is the dominion of everything, and unto Him you will be returned. (36:77-83)

In these verses, the Qur'an proves the Resurrection in seven or eight ways. First, it presents humanity's first creation and means: "You are created through the stages of a sperm-drop, something suspended on the wall of your mother's womb, something like a lump of chewed flesh, the bones and the clothing of bones in muscular tissue. As you can see this, how can you deny the other creation (the Resurrection), which is even easier than the first one?"

By reminding people of His great favors to them through *He has made for you fire out of the green tree,* Almighty God means: "The One Who bestows such favors does not leave you to yourselves, so that you enter the grave and lie there, not to be raised again."

He suggests: "You see how dead or dried trees are revived and turn green, so how can you deem it unlikely that wood-like bones will be revived? Further, is *He Who created the heavens and Earth* unable to create humanity, the fruit of the heavens and Earth? Does One Who governs a huge tree attach no importance to its fruit and leave it to others? Do you think He will leave humanity, the result of the Tree of Creation, to it own devices or to others, and thereby allow that Tree of Creation, all parts of which have been kneaded with wisdom, to go to waste?"

Again He means: "The One Who will revive you on the Day of Judgment is such that the whole universe is like an obedient soldier before Him. It submits with perfect obedience to His command of 'Be,' and it is. For Him, creating spring and a flower are equal. It is absolutely improper and irrational to see Him as impotent and challenge His Power by asking: 'Who will revive the bones?'"

Through *So glory be to Him, in Whose hand is the dominion of all things,* the Qur'an signifies: "He controls everything and has the keys to everything. He alternates night and day, and winter and summer, as easily as turning the pages of a book. He is such an All-Powerful One of Majesty that, like closing one house and opening another, He closes this world and opens the next. Given this fact and its proofs, you will be returned to Him. He will resurrect everyone and gather them in the Place of Mustering, where He will call you to account for what you did while in the world."

Such verses prepare one's mind and heart to accept the Resurrection, for they show how it resembles common things in our lives. The Qur'an sometimes mentions God's acts in the Hereafter in a similar way so that we can see the truth.

• From *suras Takwir, Infitar,* and *Inshiqaq*, respectively:

> When the sun is folded up. (81:1)
>
> When the heaven is cleft asunder. (82:1)
>
> When the heaven is split asunder. (84:1)

In these *suras*, the Qur'an describes this world's destruction and the Great Gathering in a way that we can understand. We see similar events during spring and autumn, and in earthquakes and large storms, and so can have some understanding of the events being described.

I shall point out one verse as an example: *When the rolls of pages are laid open* (81:10). This verse states that on the Day of Judgment, everyone will be confronted with a role of pages containing the record of their deeds. This is hard for us to comprehend, although we witness events every year, such as what happens during the general revival observed every spring, that are similar to the world's destruction and the Resurrection.

Every fruit-bearing tree or flowering plant has deeds, actions, and duties. Its type of worship shows the Divine Names manifested in it. All of its deeds (its life-cycle from germination to blossoming and yielding fruits) are recorded in its seeds to be exhibited in a subsequent spring on Earth. As it clearly displays the deeds of its source or origin in the tongue of its form and shape, its branches, twigs, leaves, blossoms, and fruits lay open the pages of those deeds.

Thus the One Who does this work before our eyes as displays of His Names the All-Wise, All-Preserving, All-Arranging, All-Upbringing, and All-Subtle, is He Who says: *When the rolls of pages are laid open. Compare other points with this and understand.*

Consider the explanation of: *When the sun is folded up* (81:1). Besides the brilliant metaphor in *folded up* (meaning "rolled" or "wrapped up"), the verse alludes to several related events: First, by drawing back non-existence, ether, and the skies respectively like veils, Almighty God brought a brilliant lamp (the sun) out of His Mercy's treasury to illuminate and be displayed to the world. After the world is destroyed, He will rewrap it in its veils and remove it.

Second, the sun is an official of God charged with spreading its goods of light and folding light and darkness alternately round the world's head. Each evening it gathers up and conceals its goods. Sometimes it does little business because a cloud veils it; sometimes it withdraws from doing business because the moon draws a veil over its face and closes its account book for a short, fixed time. At some [future] time, this official will resign from its post.

Even if there is no cause for its dismissal, due to the two black spots growing on its face, as they have begun to do, the sun will obey the Divine command to draw back the light it sends to the Earth and wrap it around its own head. God will order it: "You no longer have any duty toward Earth. Now, go to Hell and burn those who, by worshipping you, insulted an obedient official with disloyalty as if you had claimed divinity." Through its black-spotted face, the sun exhibits the meaning of: *When the sun is folded up.*

**NINTH POINT OF ELOQUENCE:** Sometimes the wise Qur'an mentions a particular purpose and, to urge our minds to think in universal terms, confirms and establishes that purpose through Divine Names functioning as universal rules.

• From *Surat al-Mujadila:*

> God has heard the statement of the woman who argues with you about her husband and complains unto God. God hears your conversation. God is All-Hearing, All-Seeing. (58:1)

The Qur'an says: "Almighty God is All-Hearing. He hears through His Name of Truth a wife arguing with you and complaining about her husband, a most particular matter. A woman is most compassionate among human beings, and a mine of care and tenderness leading to self-sacrifice. So, as a requirement of His being All-Compassionate, Almighty God hears her complaint and considers it a matter of great importance through His Name of Truth."

By concluding a universal principle from a particular event, One Who hears and sees a particular, minor incident must hear and see all things. One Who claims Lordship over the universe must be aware of the troubles of any creature who has been wronged and hear its cries. One Who cannot do so cannot be Lord. Thus *God is All-Hearing, All-Seeing* establishes those two mighty truths.

• From *Surat al-Isra':*

> Glorified be He Who took His servant by night from the Sacred Mosque (Masjid al-Haram) to Masjid al-Aqsa', Whose neighborhood We have blessed, that We might show him of Our signs. He is All-Hearing, All-Seeing. (17:1)

This verse relates the first stage of the Prophet's Ascension. *He* can refer to the Prophet or Almighty God. If it refers to the Prophet, it means: "This journey is a comprehensive one, a universal ascension. During it, as far as the *lote-tree of the utmost boundary* (where the Realm of the Created ends) and at a *distance of two bows' length,* he heard and saw God's signs. Amazing works of Divine art were displayed before his eyes and ears in the Divine Names' universal degrees of manifestations." Thus the verse presents this journey as the key to a universal journey.

If *He* refers to Almighty God, its means: "To admit His servant to His Presence at the end of a journey and to entrust him with a duty, He took him from Masjid al-Haram to Masjid al-Aqsa. He caused him to meet the Prophets, who were gathered there. After showing that he is the heir to the principles of all Prophets' religions, He caused him to travel through the realms of His dominion in all their inner and outer dimensions, to *the distance of two bows' length.*"

The Prophet is a servant and ascended to God's Presence. But together with him was a trust pertaining to the universe and a light that would change the universe's color. There also was a key to open the door to eternal happiness. Thus Almighty God describes Himself with the attributes of hearing and seeing all things to show the global purposes for the trust, the light, and the key.

- From *Surat al-Fatir:*

> Praise be to God, Creator of the heavens and Earth,
> Who appoints angels as messengers with wings, two,
> three, or four. He multiplies in creation as He wills.
> God is Powerful over all beings. (35:1)

This verse means: "By adorning the heavens and Earth and showing His Perfection's works, their Majestic Creator causes their innumerable spectators to extol and praise Him infinitely. He decorated them with uncountable bounties so that the heavens and Earth praise and exalt endlessly their Most Merciful Creator in the tongue of all bounties and those who receive them."

The verse also shows that the Majestic One Who has equipped all Earth's inhabitants with the necessary limbs, faculties, and wings to travel throughout the world, and Who has equipped angels (the heavens' inhabitants) with wings to fly and travel throughout the heavenly palaces of stars and lofty lands of constellations, must be powerful over all things. The One Who has given wings to a fly to fly from one fruit to another, and to a sparrow to fly from one tree to another, is He Who gives the wings with which to fly from Venus to Jupiter and from Jupiter to Saturn.

Furthermore, unlike Earth's inhabitants, angels are not restricted to particularity or confined by a specific limited space. Through *two, three, or four. He multiplies in creation as He wills,* the verse suggests that angels may be present on four or more stars at the same time. Thus by stating that God has equipped angels with wings (a particular event), the Qur'an points to the origin of a universal, tremendous power and establishes it with the summary: *God is Powerful over all things.*

**TENTH POINT OF ELOQUENCE:** Sometimes the Qur'an mentions humanity's rebellious acts and restrains its members with severe threats. But so as not to cast people into despair, it concludes with certain Divine Names pointing to His Mercy and consoles them.

- From *Surat al-Shura:*

> Say: "Had there been deities besides Him, as they say, they would certainly have sought out a way against the Lord of the Supreme Throne." Glorified is He, and high exalted above what they say. The seven heavens and Earth and all that is therein glorify Him. Everything glorifies Him with praise, but you do not understand their glorification. He is Ever-Clement, Most Forgiving. (17:42-44)

The verses mean: "Say: 'If there were deities with Him in His Sovereignty, they would have sought a share in His absolute rule over creation. This would have caused disorder in the universe. However, each part of creation glorifies the Majestic One signified by those Names in the tongue of the inscriptions of the Divine Names manifested on them. They declare Him free of any partners. Just as the heavens declare Him to be Holy and testify to His Unity through their light-diffusing worlds of suns and stars, as well as through their displayed wisdom and order, the atmosphere glorifies and sanctifies Him through the 'voice' of clouds and its words of thunder, lighting, and rain."

It also testifies to His Unity. Just as Earth glorifies its Majestic Creator and declares Him to be One through its living words of plants and animate creatures, each tree glorifies Him and testifies to His Oneness through its words of leaves, blossoms, and fruits. Likewise, even the smallest and most particular creature glorifies the All-Majestic One, many of Whose Names it displays through their inscriptions that it bears, and testifies to His Unity.

The verses state that humanity is the issue and result of the universe, its delicate fruit that has been honored with ruling Earth in God's name. However, unbelievers and those who associate partners with God (even though the universe glorifies its majestic Creator with one voice, testifies to His Oneness, and worships in perfect obedience) commit an ugly act that deserves punishment. So that such people will not give in to despair, the All-Overwhelming One of Majesty gives them time to reconsider. The concluding words of *He is Ever-Clement, Most Forgiving* leave a door open for repentance and the hope of being forgiven.

The summaries at the verses' ends contain many aspects of guidance and gleams of miraculousness. Even the greatest geniuses of eloquence have been astonished by the Qur'an's authentic forms and, concluding that it cannot have a human origin, have believed with absolute certainty that it is a Revelation revealed. Together with the points and qualities already mentioned, other verses contain many further qualities such that even the "blind" can see the impress of their miraculous arrangement.

### Third ray

The Qur'an cannot be compared with other words and speeches, for there are different categories of speech. In regard to superiority, power, beauty, and fineness, speech has four sources: the speaker, the person addressed, the purpose, and when it is spoken. Its source is not only the occasion, as some literary people have wrongly supposed. So do not consider only the speech itself.

Since speech derives its strength and beauty from these four sources, if the Qur'an's sources are studied carefully, the degree of its eloquence, superiority, and beauty will be understood. Since speech is first considered according to the speaker, if it is in the form of command and prohibition it contains a will and power proportional to the speaker's rank. Then it may be irresistible and have an effect like electricity, increasing in superiority and power.

- From *sura*s *Hud* and *Fussilat*, respectively:

  O Earth, swallow your water, and O sky, cease your rain! (11:44)

  O heaven. O Earth. Come both of you, willingly or unwillingly. They said: "We come obedient." (41:11)

That means: "O heaven and Earth, come willingly or unwillingly, and submit yourselves to
My Wisdom and Power. Come out of non-existence and appear as places where My works of
art will be shown." They replied: "We come in perfect obedience. We will carry out, by Your leave
and Power, all duties You have assigned us."

Consider the sublimity and force of those compelling commands bearing an irresistible power
and will, and think about the commands we direct
toward inanimate objects: "O Earth, stop. O heav-
en, rend asunder. O world, destroy yourself." Can
such commands be compared with His? How can
our wishes and insensible commands be compared
with the compelling commands of a supreme ruler
having all of rulership's essential qualities?

The difference between a supreme commander's compelling command to march to a mighty,
obedient army, and that of an ordinary private is
as great as the difference between the commander and the private. Consider the force and superiority of the commands in: *His command, when He
wills a thing, is to say to it "Be," and it is* (36:82),
and *When We said to the angels: "Prostrate yourselves before Adam"* (2:34) with human orders,

and see whether the difference between them is not like that between a firefly and the sun.

Consider how masters describe their work while doing it, how artists explain their artistry while working, and how benefactors discuss their goodness while doing it. We see the result of their combined actions and words. If they say that they have done that in a certain way and for a certain purpose, and in the way it must be done, you can see its difference from mere words without action.

- From *Sura Qaf:*

> Have they not observed the sky above them, how We built and adorned it? There are no rifts therein. Earth We have spread out, and have flung firm hills therein, and have caused of every lovely kind to grow thereon. A matter of insight and reflection, and a teaching and reminder for every servant who always turns to God in penitence and worship. We send down from the sky blessed water whereby We give growth unto gardens and the grain of crops, and lofty date palms with ranged clusters. Provision for the servants; and therewith We quicken a dead land. So will be the raising of the dead. (50:6-11)

The descriptions in the verses introduce, with perfect eloquence, many proofs of the Resurrection derived from the observable part of the universe, which is in action. By concluding with *So will be the raising of the dead,* they silence those whom the *sura* says deny the Resurrection. How different this is from the people's discussion of happenings with which they have little concern. The difference is greater than that between real and plastic flowers. I will interpret these verses very briefly.

The *sura* begins with the unbelievers' denial of the Resurrection. To convince them of its truth, the *sura* asks: "Don't you see how We built this ordered and magnificent sky; how We adorned it with the sun, the moon, and stars, with no rifts therein; how We spread Earth out for you, and how wisely We furnished it? Having fixed mountains thereon, We protect it against the oceans' invasion. Don't you see how We created on it all kinds of multicolored and beautiful pairs of vegetation and pasturage and then embellished Earth with them; how We send blessed water from the sky so that gardens and orchards may grow thereby, as well as grains and lofty trees like date palms bearing delicious fruits, with which We provide Our servants; how We quicken the dead soil with that water and bring about thousands of instances of resurrection? Just as We cause vegetation to grow on the dead Earth, We will resurrect you on the Day of Judgment, when Earth will die and you will rise out of it alive!"

How exalted is the eloquence displayed in these verses that prove the Resurrection, how superior to the words we use to prove a claim!

Concluding my use of objective reasoning and verification to convince unbelievers of the Qur'an's miraculousness, I point out its incomparable rank in the name of truth.

When compared with the Qur'an, all other words are like tiny reflections of stars in a glass in comparison with actual stars. In fact, how far are the meanings that human minds picture, in the mirrors of their thoughts and feelings, from the Qur'an's words, each of which describes an unchanging truth! How great is the distance between the Qur'an's angel-like, life-giving words, the Word of the Creator of the sun and moon, which also diffuses the lights of guidance, and the stinging words originated by bewitching souls and affected manners that incite desire!

When compared with the Qur'an, our words are like stinging insects in comparison with angels and other luminous spirit beings. This is not a mere assertion; rather, as is apparent in our discussions in *The Words* written so far, it is a conclusion based on evidence.

How far are our words, full of fancies and fantasies, from the Qur'an's words and phrases. This eternal Divine address, which originated from the Most Merciful One's Supreme Throne, came in consideration of humanity as an independent being superior to all other creatures, and is founded upon God's Knowledge, Power, and Will. Each word and statement is the source of a pearl of guidance and of the truths of belief, as well as the mine of an Islamic principle. How great is the distance between our familiar words and those of the Qur'an.

Like a blessed tree under which the universe lies, the Qur'an has produced the leaves of all Islamic spiritual values and moral perfections, public symbols and rules, principles and commandments. It has burst into blossoms of saints and purified scholars, and yielded fruits of Divine truths, truths and realities concerning the Divine laws of creation and the operation of the universe, and fruit pits that have grown into "trees" as principles of conduct and programs of practical life.

Every person and land has benefited from the gems of truth exhibited by the Qur'an for 14 centuries. During that time, neither too much familiarity nor the abundance of its truths, neither time's passage nor the great changes and upheavals in human life, have made people indifferent to its invaluable truths and fine, authentic styles. Nor have these things damaged or devalued them, or extinguished its beauty and freshness. This is miraculous by itself.

If someone were to claim to have produced a likeness of the Qur'an, arranged some Qur'anic truths into a book and claimed to have brought about a book similar to the Qur'an, it would be like the following:

Suppose a master-builder built a magnificent palace of various jewels, all laid in a symmetrical manner, and embellished it proportionally to each jewel's position and the palace's general design. Then imagine that an ordinary architect, knowing nothing of the palace's jewels, design, and embellishments, entered it and destroyed the master-builder's work to make it look like an ordinary building. Suppose this person hangs some beads on it that please children, and then says: "Look! I am more skillful than the original builder and have more wealth and more valuable adornments." Could anyone take such an absurd claim seriously?

**Third light**

This consists of three rays.

### First ray

A significant aspect of the Qur'an's miraculousness is explained in The Thirteenth Word. I mention it here as well, as the context makes it appropriate to do so.

To see and appreciate how each Qur'anic verse removes the darkness of unbelief by spreading the light of miraculousness and guidance, imagine yourself in pre-Islamic Arabia. During that time of ignorance and in that desert of savagery, everything was covered in veils of lifelessness and nature amid the darkness of ignorance and heedlessness.

Suddenly, you hear from the Qur'an's sublime tongue such verses as: *All that is in the heavens and Earth glorifies God, the Sovereign, All-Holy, All-Mighty, All-Wise* (62:1). See how the world's lifeless or sleeping creatures spring to life in the minds of the audience at the sound of glorifies, how they wake, spring up, and begin to extol God by mentioning His Names.

At the sound of: *The seven heavens and Earth glorify Him* (17:44), the stars in that black sky, each a solid piece of fire, and Earth's creatures present to the audience the sky like a mouth; and the stars, each like a wisdom-displaying word, a truth-showing light; and Earth like a head with the land and sea, each a tongue; and all animals and plants as words of glorification. If you look at each verse in the present context and from a "modern" viewpoint,[36] if you look at it through a superficial veil of familiarity, you will neither see what sort of darkness each verse removes in a sweet melody of miraculousness nor appreciate this aspect of its miraculousness.

If you would like to see one of the highest degrees of the Qur'an's miraculousness, consider the following parable:

---

[36] In other words, after each has spread its light since its revelation, with its content having long since become among the already known things after having long ago changed the heavy darkness of ignorance into daylight by the "sun" of the Qur'an and the light of Islam.

Imagine a vast, spreading tree hidden under a veil of the Unseen. There is a relationship, harmony, and balance between all its parts, just as there is between the parts of human body. Each part assumes a form and a shape according to the tree's nature. If someone draws a picture corresponding exactly to that hidden tree, giving each part its exact shape and form, as well as the exact same relationship and proportion as seen in the original, no one can doubt that the artist sees and depicts the hidden tree with an eye penetrating the Unseen.

In the same way, the Qur'an's explanations of the reality of things cannot be refuted. It explains the Tree of Creation as stretching from the world's beginning to the Hereafter's furthest limits, spreading from Earth to the Divine Throne, and from atoms to the sun. It maintains the proportion between all parts to such a degree, and gives each part and fruit such a suitable form that all exacting and truth-seeking scholars have concluded: "What wonders God has willed. May God bless it. Only you, O wise Qur'an, solve the mystery of creation."

Let's represent God's Names and Attributes, as well as His Lordship's acts, as a great tree of light stretching in time and space to eternity. It includes the actions in an endlessly vast sphere from eternity, as well as the actions in an endlessly vast sphere from: *He comes between humanity and a person's heart* (8:24), *The Splitter of the seed-grain and the date-stone* (6:95), and *He fashions you in the wombs as He wills* (3:6) to *And the heavens rolled up in His right hand* (39:67), *He created the heavens and Earth in 6 days*. . . and *He has subjugated the sun and the moon* (7:154).

The wise Qur'an describes that radiant reality, the truths of those Names and Attributes, as well as of those acts in all of their ramifications and results, so harmoniously and appropriately that no item impedes or invalidates the decree of another. All who have penetrated the reality of things and discovered the hidden truths, and all sages journeying in the Realm of the Inner Dimension of Things, have declared of this description: "Glory be to God. How right, how conformable with reality, how beautiful, how fitting."

Consider the six pillars of belief, which are like a branch of two mighty trees—the Sphere of Contingency (material existence) and the Sphere of Necessity (Divine Existence). The Qur'an describes all parts of that branch. The arrangement of all parts is so harmonious, balanced, and well-measured that the human mind cannot perceive it; rather, it is astonished at its beauty. The Qur'an has established a beautiful proportion, perfect relationship, and complete balance between the five pillars of Islam (which are like a twig of the branch of belief), between the finest details (e.g., the least of good manners) and the furthest aims, and between the most profound wisdom and the most minor fruits.

The perfect order, balance, proportion, and soundness seen in the Shari'a, which originated from the all-comprehensive Qur'an's incontrovertible Commandments, as well as the secondary meanings, indications, and allusions of its statements, are an irrefutable, decisive proof and a just, undeniable witness for that proportion, balance, order, and soundness.

Thus its explanations cannot have issued from anyone's partial knowledge, particularly an unlettered person. Rather, they issued from an All-Comprehensive Knowledge and are the Word of One Who can see all things together like a single thing and simultaneously observe all truths between two eternities. *Praise be to God Who has sent down unto His servant the Book, and has allowed no crookedness therein* (18:1) concerns this fact.

## Second ray

The Twelfth and other Words discussed to what extent human philosophy is inferior to the Qur'an's wisdom. Here we compare them from another perspective.

Philosophy and science view existence as permanent and discuss creatures' nature and qualities in detail. If they mention their duties toward their Creator at all, they do so only very briefly, as if they discuss only the designs and letters of the Book of the Universe and ignore its meaning. But since the Qur'an views existence as transient, moving, illusory, unstable, and changing, it mentions all creatures' nature and outward, physical qualities rather briefly and spends a great deal of time elaborating the duties of worship with which their Creator has charged them, the ways they manifest His Names, and their submission to the Divine laws of creation and operation of the universe. Thus, in order to distinguish truth from falsehood, we should see the differences between human philosophy and Qur'anic wisdom related to summarizing and elaborating.

However unmoving, constant, and static a clock outwardly appears, it is in a state of continuous movement in essence and inwardly. Likewise the world, which is a huge clock of the Divine Power, rolls or revolves unceasingly in continuous change and upheaval. Its two "hands" of night and day show the passage of its seconds, and its "hands" of years and centuries show the passage of its minutes and hours. Time plunges the world into waves of decay and, leaving the past and future to non-existence, allows existence for the present only.

The world also is changing and unstable with respect to space. Its atmosphere changes rapidly, filling with and being cleared of clouds several times a day and displaying weather-related changes. Such activity corresponds to the passage of seconds. Earth, the world's floor, undergoes continuous change through cycles of life and death and in vegetation and animals. Such cycles correspond to the passage of minutes and demonstrate the world's transience.

Such cycles can be found in Earth's interior, where convulsions and upheavals cause such events as earthquakes and the emergence and subsidence

of mountains. These are like an hour hand showing the world's mortality. The movements of heavenly bodies in the sky (the world's roof), the appearance of comets and new stars while some others
are extinguished, as well as solar and lunar eclipses,
demonstrate that it is not stable and therefore is
making its way toward a final ruin. However slow
its changes are, they also show that the world is
mortal and moves to its inevitable end.

The "pillars" upon which this world was built
shake it continually. When considered with respect
to its Maker, whose movements and changes are
the results of the movements of the Divine Power's
Pen writing the Eternally-Besought-of-All's mis-
sives, this world and its transformations function
as ever-renewed or ever-polished mirrors reflecting the Divine Names' manifestations in all different aspects. Thus, when considered with respect to
itself and being a material, created entity, the world
continually convulses and moves toward decay and
death.

Although the world moves like flowing water,
heedlessness has frozen it and (philosophical) naturalism has solidified it so that it has become a veil
that conceals and makes one forget the afterlife.

Philosophy is nourished by modern scientific thought and supported by corrupt modern civilization's alluring amusements and the intoxicating desires it arouses in people. Such things make the world more turbid and increase its solidity, which causes people to forget the Creator and the afterlife.

Through such verses as: *The calamity. What is the calamity?* (101:1-2); *When the inevitable event befalls* (56:1); and *By the Mount, and a Scripture inscribed* (52:1-2), the Qur'an shatters this world and cards it like wool. Through such verses as: *Have they not considered the dominion and inner aspect of the heavens and Earth?* (7:185); *Have they not then observed the sky above them, how We have made it?* (50:6); and: *Did not the unbelievers know that the heavens and Earth were of one piece, then We parted them?* (21:30), it gives that world a transparency and removes its turbidity. Through its bright, light-diffusing "stars" like: *God is the Light of the heavens and Earth* (24:35) and: *The life of this world is but a play and amusement* (6:32), it melts that solid world.

Through its threatening verses that recall death, such as: *When the sun is folded up* (81:1), *When the heaven is cleft asunder* (82:1), *When the heav-*

*en is split asunder* (84:1), and *The Trumpet is blown, and all who are in the heavens and on Earth fall down senseless, save those whom God wills* (39:68), it destroys the delusion that the world is eternal. Through its thunder-like blasts, such as: *He knows all that enters Earth and all that emerges therefrom and all that comes down from the heaven and all that ascends therein. He is with you wherever you may be. God sees all that you do* (57:4) and *Say: "Praise be to God, Who will show you His signs so that you shall know them. Your Lord is not unaware of what you do"* (27:93), it removes heedlessness, which gives rise to naturalism.

Thus those Qur'anic verses concerned with the universe follow the principle outlined above. They unveil the world's reality and display it as it is. By showing the world's ugly face, it turns us away from it; by pointing out its beautiful face, which is turned toward the Maker, it turns our face toward it. It instructs us in true wisdom and teaches us the meanings of the Book of the Universe, with little attention to its letters and decorations. Unlike human philosophy, it does not give itself over to what is ugly and, causing people to forget the meaning, lead them to waste their time on such meaningless things as the letters' decorations.

## Third ray

In the Second Ray, we pointed out the inferiority of human philosophy to the Qur'an's wisdom as well as the latter's miraculousness. In this Ray, which compares the Qur'an's wisdom with the philosophy of its students (e.g., purified scholars, saints, and the Illuminists [the more enlightened class of philosophers]), we will discuss briefly the Qur'an's miraculousness in this respect.

We now present a most true evidence for its nobility, the clearest proof of its truth, and a most powerful sign of its miraculousness. Consider this: The Qur'an contains and explains all degrees, varieties, and requirements of Divine Unity's manifestation in a perfectly balanced manner.[37] Moreover, it maintains the equilibrium among elevated Divine truths, contains all commandments and principles required by the Divine Names, and maintains exact

_____

[37] For example, Unity of Divine Being, and being unique or having no matches in His Essential Qualities as being God and the Lord, and in His Attributes, Names, and acts. (Tr.)

and sensitive relationships among them. It holds together all the acts and "functions" of God's Divinity and Lordship with perfect balance.

All of these show its matchless virtue and characteristics, which cannot be found in the greatest human works, in those of saints who penetrate the inner realities of things, or of those Illuminists who discern the inner aspects of things and events, or of those wholly purified scholars who penetrate the World of the Unseen. It is as if, according to a certain division of labor, each group devoted itself to one branch of the mighty tree of truth and busied itself only with its leaves and fruits, all the while being unaware of the others.

Absolute, unlimited truth cannot be comprehended by restricted minds and vision, but only by the Qur'an's universal and all-encompassing vision. All that is not the Qur'an cannot comprehend the universal truth in its entirety, even if they benefit from it, for their minds are limited, restricted, and wholly absorbed in only a couple of its parts. They frequently go to extremes, dwelling on one or two points more than the others, and thereby destroy the balance and accurate relations among the truths. This point was discussed in the Second Branch of The Twenty-fourth Word. We will approach it here with another parable.

Imagine a treasure under the sea full of jewels. Many divers look for it but, since their eyes are closed, they search for it with their hands. One seizes a large diamond and concludes that he[38] has found the treasure. When he hears that his friends have found other jewels, such as a round ruby or a square amber, he thinks that they are facets or embellishments of what he has found. Each diver has the same idea.

---

[38] God declares in the Qur'an: *I shall not allow to go to waste the deed of any one of you, whether male or female. You are one from the other* (3:195). Islam does not discriminate between men and women in religious responsibility. Each gender shares most of the responsibilities, but each one has certain responsibilities that are particular to it. The Qur'an usually uses the masculine form of address, for this is one of Arabic's characteristics. In almost every language, the masculine form is used for a group comprising both men and women, like the English word *mankind*, which includes both men and women. So, brotherhood also includes sisterhood, and, since the believers comprise both male and female believers, the believers are brothers and sisters. However, in order to maintain the original text and avoid repetition, usually we do not mention the feminine forms in translation. (Tr.)

Such a thought and attitude destroys the balance and accurate relations among truths. It even changes the color of many of them, for one is compelled to make forced interpretations and detailed explanations to see the true color of truths or show them to others. Some even deny or falsify them.

Those who carefully study the Illuminists' books or those of Sufi masters who rely on their visions and illuminations without weighing them on the scales of the Qur'an and the Sunna will confirm this judgment. Although they have benefited from the Qur'an and generally have been taught by it, their teachings have certain shortcomings and defects because they are not the Qur'an itself. The Qur'an, that ocean of truths, encompasses and sees in its verses the entire treasure and describes its jewels in such a harmonious and balanced way that they show their beauty perfectly.

For example, just as the Qur'an sees and shows the Divine Lordship's grandeur in: *The whole Earth is His handful on the Day of this world's destruction and building of the next, and the heavens are rolled up in His Right Hand* (39:67) and *The day when We shall roll up the heavens like a scroll rolled up for books* (21:104), it sees and shows the all-encompassing Mercy expressed by God: *nothing on Earth or in the heavens is hidden from Him. He shapes you in the wombs as He pleases* (3:5-6); *He grasps every moving creature by the forelock* (11:56), and *How many a moving creature there is that bears not its own provision. God provides for it and for you* (29:60).

Just as it sees and points out the vast creativity expressed by: *(He) has created the heavens and Earth and made the darkness and the light* (6:1), it sees and shows the comprehensive Divine control of things and His encompassing Lordship in: *He creates you and what you do* (37:96). It sees and shows the mighty truth expressed in: *He gives life to Earth after its death* (30:50) and the truth concerning His munificence expressed in: *Your Lord has inspired the bee* (16:68), and the great truth concerning His Sovereignty and command expressed in: *The sun and the moon and the stars subservient by His command* (7:54).

The Qur'an sees and shows the truth of compassion and administration expressed in: *Do they not observe the birds above them in ranks, spreading and closing their wings? None upholds them save the Most Merciful; indeed He sees all things*

(67:19); the vast truth expressed in: *His Seat includes the heavens and Earth, and He is never weary of preserving them* (2:255); the truth concerning His overseeing, expressed by: *He is with you wheresoever you may be* (57:4); the all-embracing truth expressed by: *He is the First and the Last, the Outward and the Inward, and knows all things* (57:3); His being nearer to beings than themselves, expressed by: *We have created humanity and know what its soul whispers to it; We are nearer to humanity than its jugular vein* (50:16); the elevated truth expressed by: *The angels and the Spirit ascend to Him in a day the span of which is 50,000 years* (70:4); and the all-encompassing truth expressed by: *God enjoins justice and absolute kindness, and giving to kinsfolk, and forbids all shameful deeds, things abominable to sound conscience, injustice and rebellion* (16:90).

In short, the Qur'an sees and shows in detail all truths pertaining to knowledge and practice concerning this world and the next, and each of the six pillars of belief. It points out purposefully and earnestly each of the five pillars of Islam and all other principles of securing happiness in both worlds. It preserves the exact balance and

maintains the accurate relationship and proportion among them. The subtlety and beauty originating from the harmony of the entirety of those
truths give rise to a form of the Qur'an's miraculousness.

Theologians study the Qur'an and have written
many volumes on the pillars of belief. But some
of them, like the Mu'tazilites, have preferred reason over transmitted knowledge originating from
Divine Revelations and so have not been able to
explain these truths as effectively as even 10
Qur'anic verses. It is as though they have dug tun-
nels under mountains as far as the end of the world
to obtain and convey water. They have gone along
with the chains of cause and effect as far as the
beginning of time and then, cutting the chains,
jumped over to eternity to obtain the knowledge
of God (the water of life for people) and prove the
Necessarily Existent One's Existence.

On the other hand, each Qur'anic verse can
extract "water" from every place like the staff of
Moses, opening up a window from everything and
making the Majestic Maker known. In addition,
because they could not preserve the exact balance
between the truths, leaders of all heretical groups,

those who have delved into the inner nature of things by relying on their visions instead of the Prophet's Sunna,[39] have returned half-way and formed different sects. This caused them to fall into heresy and misguidance, and to cause others to deviate. Their failure also demonstrates the Qur'an's miraculousness.

## Conclusion

Among the gleams of the Qur'an's miraculousness, its reiterations and brief mentions of scientific facts and developments, which are wrongly thought to be a cause of defects, were discussed in the Fourteenth Droplet of The Nineteenth Word. Another gleam of the Qur'an's miraculousness, radiating in its mention of the Prophets' miracles, was shown in the Second Station of The Twentieth

---

[39] The Sunna is the record of the Messenger's every act, word, and confirmation, as well as the second source of Islamic legislation and life (the Qur'an is the first one). In addition to establishing new principles and rules, the Sunna clarifies the ambiguities in the Qur'an by expanding upon what is mentioned only briefly in it, specifies what is unconditional, and enables generalizations from what is specifically stated and particularizations from what is generally stated. (Ed.)

Word. You will find many other gleams discussed in other Words and my Arabic treatises. However, I will add here another aspect.

Just as the Prophets' miracles exhibit an aspect of the Qur'an's miraculousness, the Qur'an with all its miracles is a miracle of Muhammad, and all of his miracles constitute a miracle of the Qur'an. They demonstrate its Divine authorship, through which each word becomes a miracle, for just like a seed, each word may contain a tree of truths; just like a heart's center, it may have relations with all parts of a mighty truth.

Since it depends on an All-Encompassing Knowledge and Infinite Will, it may be interrelated via its letters, position, meaning, connotations, and in its entirety, with countless other things. This is why specialists in the science of letters assert that each letter of the Qur'an contains as many mysteries as may cover a page, and prove it to those who have expert knowledge in that science.

Consider all the Lights, Rays, Gleams, Radiances, and Beams discussed so far, and see how the claim at the beginning becomes a decisive, undeniable conclusion. In other words, this entire treatise decisively proclaims the truth of: *Say: "If humanity and jinn banded together to produce the like of this Qur'an, they would never produce its like, even though they backed one another"* (17:88).

Glory be to You. We have no knowledge save what You have taught us. You are the All-Knowing, All-Wise. Our Lord, do not reproach us if we forget or make mistakes. Lord, open my breast and make my task easy. Loosen a knot on my tongue so that they can understand my words.

O God, bestow blessings and peace; the best, finest, most pleasant and most manifest, purest, most gracious and most abundant, mightiest, greatest, most honored and most elevated, most flourishing and most prosperous, and the most subtle of your blessings; the most sufficient and most abundant, most ample and most exalted, most sublime and most constant of Your peace; and as blessing, peace, mercy, good pleasure, forgiving, and pardoning, in increase and continuity along with the rains from the clouds as favors of Your Generosity and Munificence, and in continuos multiplication along with the fine and exquisite bounties of Your Generosity and Benevolence; eternally, without beginning or end, along with Your eternity—on Your servant, Your beloved, and Your Messenger, Muhammad, the best of Your creatures, the brightest light, the clearest and most decisive proof, the most profound ocean, the most comprehensive light, having shone grace and overwhelming majesty and superior perfection; bestow blessings on him through the grandeur of Your Being, and blessings on his Family and Companions through which You may forgive our sins, open our breasts, purify our hearts, uplift our spirits, bless us, refine our memories and thoughts, remove the filth from our souls, cure us of our diseases, and open the locks on our hearts.

## First addendum

A person searching for his Lord said to himself: "Let's look at the book called the Qur'an of miraculous exposition, which is said to be the Word of the One I have been searching for and challenges its opponents. Let's see what it says about the Lord. Is it really a Divine Book, the Book of the Creator, as is claimed?"

Since he lives in this age, first he inquired of the *Risale-i Nur* about the Creator. Seeing that its 130 treatises comprise the explanations and substantial interpretations of certain Qur'anic truths, he understood from its content and forceful diffusing and defending of the Qur'anic truths in this age of unbelief that the Qur'an is a revealed book. Especially after reading the Eighteenth Sign of The Nineteenth Letter and The Twenty-fifth Word, which convincingly argue that the Qur'an is a miracle in 40 respects, he almost was convinced of its Divine authorship and noticed a few more points showing its excellence:

## Six points

**FIRST POINT:** With all the aspects of its miraculousness and the truths it contains, which prove its truth, the Qur'an is a miracle of Muhammad. In the same way the Prophet, with all his miracles and his Prophethood's proofs, as well as his perfect knowledge and integrated personality, is a miracle of the Qur'an and a decisive proof of its Divine authorship.

**SECOND POINT:** The Qur'an brought about a substantial, happy, and enlightening change in the social life of a considerable portion of humanity. In addition, it continues to bring about such a revolution in people's souls, hearts, and intellects, as well as in their personal, social, and political lives. Its more than 6,600 verses, which have been recited in utmost respect by countless people for centuries, continue to educate people spiritually and intellectually, purify souls, refine intellects, uplift and expand spirits, guide to truth and sound thinking, and make people happy. Such a book must be miraculous, genuine, extraordinary, and unequaled.

**THIRD POINT:** From the first day, the Qur'an's eloquence has captivated literary people. For example, it dimmed the Seven Poems.[40] While removing her father's poem from the wall, Labid's daughter remarked: "After the revelation of the Qur'an, this has no value." On hearing: *Proclaim openly and insistently what you are commanded* (15:94), a Bedouin prostrated. When asked if he had become a Muslim, he said: "No. I prostrated before this verse's eloquence."

Many geniuses of literature and the science of eloquence, like 'Abd al-Qahir al-Jurjani, al-Sakkaki, and al-Zamakhshari, have concluded that the Qur'an's eloquence is unequaled. Moreover, it has challenged all geniuses of literature and eloquence to dispute with it: "Either produce a single *sura* like mine, or suffer humiliation and ruin in both worlds by denying me." The unbelieving literary people of the Prophet's time could not meet this

---

[40] Known as the Seven Suspended Poems because they were written in gold and hung up on the Ka'ba's wall prior to the Qur'an's revelation.

challenge, and so took up arms against him. This proves that any dispute with the Qur'an is futile.

Countless books in Arabic have been written by friends of the Qur'an who seek to imitate it and by its enemies who criticize it. Anyone, even the simplest person, who hears the Qur'an will conclude that it is superior to all human works. No other book even comes close to resembling it. This leaves us with two options: either it is inferior or superior to all other books. As no one can honestly claim that it is inferior, it must be superior.

Once someone recited: *All that is in the heavens and Earth glorifies God* (57:1), and remarked: "I cannot find in this verse such extraordinary eloquence as the Qur'an is claimed to have." He was told: "Go to pre-Islamic Arabia [or another place where the darkness of atheism or materialism prevails] and listen to this verse." The man imagined that he was living in pre-Islamic Arabia [or the world of, say, existentialist philosophers]. He saw that all creatures were leading purposeless, wretched, and meaningless lives. In this dark, unstable, and transient world they were travelling aimlessly in a dark, boundless space devoid of meaning.

Suddenly he heard this verse from the tongue of the Qur'an. He saw that it removed the dark veil from the world's face, illuminating it so much that the eternal sermon and everlasting decree was teaching all conscious beings, lined up in the rows of centuries. It was showing them that the universe is like a huge mosque in which all creatures, including the heavens and Earth, continually glorify, praise, and invoke Him in rapture and utmost happiness.

Then, tasting this verse's eloquence and comparing it with others, he understood one of the infinite reasons why the Qur'an's resonating and reverberating eloquence has conquered one-fifth of humanity and has maintained its majestic dominion for 14 centuries.

**FOURTH POINT:** The Qur'an has a sweetness that, despite repeated recitation, never bores people; rather, it gives increasing pleasure. It maintains its freshness and originality as if newly revealed, despite its easy availability, widespread memorization, and its 14 centuries of age. Every age feels as if the Qur'an is addressing it directly. Although all scholars have had frequent recourse to it in every age and have always benefited from it, and although they usually have followed its styles of expression, it still preserves its authentic styles and forms of explanation.

**FIFTH POINT:** The Qur'an is rooted deeply in the unchanging truths on which all previous Prophets agree. It confirms them, and they affirm it by agreeing on its truths. All of its fruits (e.g., Islamic sciences and spiritual disciplines of sainthood), which originated from it and showed that each is a blessed, living tree yielding fruits of enlightening truths, state that the Qur'an is truth itself and a collection of truths unequaled in comprehensiveness.

**SIXTH POINT:** All six sides or aspects of the Qur'an are luminous and demonstrate its truth. From below, it is supported upon the pillars of proof and evidence [e.g., rational, scientific, historical, those pertaining to conscience and sound judgment]; above it are gleams of the seal of miraculousness, before it lies happiness in both worlds as its aim; and behind it is another point of support: the truths of Divine Revelation. To its right is the unanimous confirmation of guided reason based on proofs, and to its left are the intellectual and spiritual contentment of those with sound hearts and conscience, and their sincere attachment and submission to it.

All of these bear witness that the Qur'an is a formidable, extraordinary, and unconquerable stronghold established by the hand of heaven on Earth. They set their seal of admission that it is a faultless, true Word of God. The Administrator of the universe, Who always manifests unity, protects virtuousness and goodness, and extirpates falsehood and slander, has given the Qur'an the most acceptable, high, and dominant rank of respect and success. Given this, God Himself has confirmed its truth.

Also the Prophet, the Qur'an's interpreter, believed in and respected it more than anything and anybody clse. He went into a different state when its verses were being revealed, and confirmed and preached all its decrees and commandments with utmost conviction, without showing any deception and error to those waiting to catch him, and without anything to shake him. Despite being unlettered, the Qur'an enabled him to relate instantly what was revealed about the past and future, the facts of creation and the universe's operation. Other sayings of his do not resemble the Qur'an and are inferior to it in certain respects. All of this proves that the Qur'an is the true heavenly and blessed Word of his Merciful Creator.

One-fifth of humanity, or even the majority of people in certain cases, always have had an ecstatic and religious devotion to the Qur'an. They listened to it lovingly and in adoration of truth, and as testified to by numerous observations, signs, and events. Just as moths fly round a light, angels, believing jinn, and other spirit beings gather around the Qur'an during its recitation. This also confirms that the Qur'an is accepted by almost all beings in the universe and that it is of the highest rank.

All types of people derive their share from its teachings. The greatest scholars in Islamic sciences (e.g., jurisprudence, theology, and religious methodology) have found in it answers to their questions and so have based their conclusions upon it. This is another evidence that the Qur'an is the source of truths, the mine of all true knowledge. Furthermore, no unbelieving Arab literary genius ever has produced anything like it. Other geniuses of learning and eloquence who sought to produce something as eloquent as the Qur'an have been compelled to refrain from doing so. This clearly shows that the Qur'an is a miracle.

To judge a word's value, sublimity, and eloquence, we must ask who spoke it, to whom was it spoken, and why was it spoken. When considered in this way, the Qur'an has no equal, for it is the Word of the Lord of all beings, the Speech of the Creator of the universe. Nothing in it suggests that it has been fabricated by someone and then falsely attributed to God.

God revealed the Qur'an to His chosen representative of all creatures, one who is His most famous and renowned addressee, whose belief embraced the comprehensive religion of Islam and caused its owner to rise to the rank of the *distance of two bows' length.* After being honored with direct conversation with the Eternally-Besought-of-All, he returned to convey the principles of happiness in both worlds.

The Qur'an explains these principles, as well as the results of and the Divine purpose in creating the universe. It expounds upon the Prophet's most comprehensive belief, which sustains all the truths of Islam. It shows and describes the universe as a map, a clock, or a house, and teaches about the Artist Who made it. It cannot be matched or equaled in any respect.

In addition, numerous Qur'anic interpretations written by meticulous scholars of the highest intelligence and learning present proofs for countless virtues, subtleties, and mysteries of the Qur'an, and disclose and affirm its numerous predictions. Among them, the *Risale-i Nur's* 130 treatises explain each Qur'anic virtue and subtlety, as can be seen throughout *The Words*. All of this sets a seal on the fact that the Qur'an is a miracle, has no equal, and is the Word of the Knower of the Unseen, which is the tongue of the World of the Unseen in this material world.

Due to its virtues, the Qur'an's magnificent spiritual dominion and majestic sacred rule continue to illuminate Earth and the ages, as well as time and space, and more people are embracing it with perfect respect. Due to these same virtues, each letter yields at least 10 merits, 10 rewards, and 10 fruits pertaining to the eternal world, and the letters of certain verses and *sura*s each give hundreds or even thousands of merits. When recited on certain blessed occasions, the light and merits of each letter multiply by tens or hundreds.

The world-traveler came to understand this and said to himself or herself: "Based on the consensus of its lights and mysteries, and the concord of its fruits and results, this Qur'an, miraculous in every respect, proves and testifies to the Existence, Unity, Attributes, and Names of a single Necessarily Existent One in such a manner that the testimonies of innumerable believers have their sources in that testimony."

In a brief reference to the instruction the traveler received from the Qur'an about belief and God's Unity, we say: "There is no god but God—the Necessarily Existent One, the One, the Single—the necessity of Whose existence in His Oneness is proved decisively by the Qur'an of miraculous exposition." This is accepted and sought for by angels, people, and jinn.

All of its verses are recited every minute and with perfect respect by countless people. Its sacred rule has prevailed in various regions of the Earth, realms of space, and on the faces of all ages and time. Its enlightened spiritual dominion has prevailed with perfect splendor over one-fifth of humanity for 1,400 years. Likewise, with the consensus of its heavenly and sacred *sura*s, the agreement of its luminous Divine verses, the correspondence of its mysteries and lights, the concord of its truths, and its results, it manifestly attests to and is a clear proof of this same truth.

## The flower of Emirdag[41]

The following is a persuasive response to the objections raised about repetitions in the Qur'an.

My dear, faithful brothers (and sisters). Confused and ill-expressed though it is—because of my distressing situation—the following is a reflection on an aspect of the Qur'an's miraculousness. Unfortunately, I cannot put it into [proper] words. However poor in wording, because it deals with the Qur'an it will lead to reflection. It may be likened to the wrapper over a bright, invaluable gem. So consider the gem being offered, not its ragged covering. I wrote it swiftly and concisely, during a few days in Ramadan while I was very ill and malnourished. Please forgive any shortcomings.

My dear, faithful brothers (and sisters). The Qur'an issues, first of all, from the greatest and most comprehensive rank of the Eternal Speaker's uni-

---

[41] A mountainous district of Afyon province (western Turkey) where Said Nursi was kept under surveillance for years. (Tr.)

versal Lordship. It is addressed, first of all, to the comprehensive rank of the one who received it in the name of the universe. Its purpose is to guide humanity from the time of its revelation until the end of time. It therefore contains entirely meaningful and comprehensive explanations about the Lordship of the Creator of the universe, Who is the Lord of this world and the Hereafter, Earth and the heavens, and eternity; and about the Divine laws pertaining to the administration of all creatures.

This discourse is so comprehensive and elevated, and therefore so inclusive and miraculous, that both the simplest (the majority) and the most intelligent (the minority) people are perfectly satisfied with what it says. It addresses and is revealed to every age and all levels of understanding and learning not as a collection of historical stories to give lessons, but as a collection of universal principles. While describing the punishments of the people of 'Ad and Thamud and Pharaoh for their sins, and with its severe threats against wrongdoers, it warns all tyrants and criminals, especially those of our own time, of the consequences of their tyranny and wrongdoing. By mentioning the final triumphs of such Prophets as Abraham and Moses, it consoles wronged believers.

The Qur'an of miraculous expression revives the past, which, in the view of heedlessness and misguidance, is a lonely and frightful realm, a dark and ruined cemetery. It transforms the past into living pages of instructions, a wondrous animated realm under the Lord's direct control, a realm that has significant relations with us. By transporting us back to those times or displaying them to us, the Qur'an teaches us in its elevated miraculous style.

In the same style, it shows the universe's true nature. The misguided see it as an unending, lifeless, lonely, and frightful place rolling in decay and separations, while believers see it as a book of the Eternally-Besought-of-All, a city of the Most Merciful One, a place to exhibit the works of the Lord's art. In it, lifeless objects become animate beings performing their particular duties and helping one another in a perfect system of communication.

This most glorious Qur'an, which enlightens and instructs angels, jinn, and humanity most pleasingly in Divine Wisdom, has such sacred distinctions as: each letter brings an unknown number of merits; all jinn or humanity, even if they joined together, cannot produce something equal to the Qur'an; it speaks to all people and the universe in the most proper way, and is continuously inscribed easily and pleasantly in the minds of millions of people; however frequently it is recited, it never bores or tires; despite its similar sentences and phrases that might cause confusion, children can memorize it easily; and it gives pleasure and tranquillity to the sick and the dying, for whom listening to even a few [human] words causes great discomfort. The Qur'an causes its students to gain happiness in both worlds.

Observing the illiteracy of the one who brought it, and without giving itself unnecessary trouble and becoming pretentious or ostentatious, the Qur'an preserves its stylistic fluency and purity and never ignores the level of understanding of the most common people. Also, it instructs people in the wisdom and extraordinary miracles of the Divine Power lying under all familiar events in the heavens and Earth, and thereby displays a fine aspect of miraculousness within the grace of its guidance.

The Qur'an shows that it is a book of supplication and invocation, a call to eternal salvation, and a declaration of God's Unity, all of which require reiteration. Therefore it repeats one sentence or story, gives numerous meanings to many different groups or categories of addressees, treats with compassion even the smallest and slightest things and events, and includes them in the sphere of its will and control. It seeks to present universal principles by paying attention to particular events, related to the Companions, that are connected with establishing Islam and legislating its laws and like seeds, thereby producing many important fruits. All of this constitutes another aspect of its miraculousness.

The repetition of needs requires reiteration. Also, the Qur'an answers many questions asked repeatedly during the 23 years of its revelation and seeks to satisfy all levels of understanding and learning. To prove that all things are controlled by a Single One Who will destroy the universe and replace it with the extraordinary world of the Hereafter, and to establish a mighty and all-comprehensive revolution in human minds that will show the Divine rage and wrath in the name of the results of the universe's creation and in the face of human injustice and wrongdoing that anger and bring the universe, Earth, and the heavens to fury, the Qur'an repeats some sentences and verses.

These are the conclusions of innumerable proofs and have a weight as great as that of thousands of conclusions. So, making repetitions for these purposes must be—and is—an extremely powerful aspect of miraculousness, an extremely elevated virtue of eloquence, and a beauty of language in conformity with the subject matter's requirements.

For example, as is explained in the Fourteenth Gleam of the *Risale-i Nur* and included in The First Word, *In the Name of God, the Merciful, the Compassionate,* which comes at the beginning of every *sura* (except one) and—together with that in *Surat al-Naml*—is repeated 114 times, is a truth linking the Earth to God's Supreme Throne and all spheres of the universe, and illuminating the universe. As everybody is in constant need of this, it is worth repeating millions of times. We need it not only every day like bread, but at every moment, just as we need air and light.

*Your Lord is He Who is the All-Honorable with an irresistible might, the All-Compassionate,* which has the strength of thousands of truths, is repeated eight times in *Surat al-Shu'ara'*, which tells of the Prophets' final triumph and salvation and their rebellious peoples' ruin. If, on behalf of the results of the universe's creation, in the name of God's universal Lordship, and to instruct people therein, and whereas the Lord's Might and Dignity require the wrongdoers' ruin and His Compassion demands the Prophets' triumph and salvation, this sentence were repeated thousands of times, there still would be a need for it. It would be a concise and miraculous aspect of the Qur'an's eloquence.

*Which of Your Lord's bounties will you two deny?* (55:13) and *Woe on that day to the deniers* (77:15), which are repeated several times in their respective *sura*s, exclaim before Earth, the heavens, the ages, and in the face of humanity and jinn, their ingratitude, unbelief, and wrongdoing. They also proclaim their violation of the rights of all creatures, which brings the heavens and Earth to rage, spoils the results of the universe's creation, and indicates contempt and denial of Divine Sovereignty's majesty. If these two verses were repeated thousands of times, in a universal teaching related to thousands of issues, a need for them still would remain.

It would be a conciseness in majesty and a miraculousness of eloquence in grace and beauty.

*Al-Jawshan al-Kabir,* a well-known supplication of the Prophet derived from the Qur'an, consists of 100 sections. Each section ends with: *Glory be to You. There is no god but You, the Protector, One in Whom refuge is sought. Save us from the Fire.* These sentences affirm God's Unity, the greatest truth in the universe. They also show three mighty duties of all created beings toward the Lord. These are the following: glorification, praise, holding Him to be All-Holy and free of defect, exalted above what polytheists wrongly attribute to Him; a supplication for humanity to be saved from eternal punishment (our most vital concern); and an aspect of our servanthood to God (the most necessary result of our helplessness before God). Thus it would be insufficient even if repeated thousands of times.

The Qur'an makes reiterations because of such essential needs and realities. As required by the occasion, demanded by eloquence, and to facilitate understanding, it sometimes expresses the truth of Divine Unity 20 times in one page, whether explicitly or implicitly. It does not bore; rather, it enforces the meaning and encourages.

*Sura*s revealed in Makka and Madina differ from each other in eloquence and miraculousness, elaboration or conciseness, for the Makkans were mainly Qurayshi polytheists. Given this, the Qur'an had to use forceful, eloquent, and concise language with an elevated style, and reiterate certain points to establish its truths.

The Makkan *sura*s repeatedly express the pillars of belief and the forms or categories of Divine Unity in a forceful, emphatic, concise, and miraculous language. They do so not only in one page, verse, sentence, or word, but also in one letter, changing the word order, using (or not using) definite articles, or mentioning or omitting certain words, phrases, and sentences. They prove the world's beginning and end, the Divine Being, and the Hereafter in so powerful a way that geniuses of the science of eloquence have been amazed.

The Makkan *sura*s' most elevated eloquence and miraculous conciseness are discussed in The Twenty-fifth Word and my *Isharat al-I'jaz,* which explain 40 aspects of the Qur'an's miraculousness and its miraculous wording.

The *sura*s revealed in Madina, during Islam's second phase, mainly address believers, Jews, and Christians. As required by circumstance, guidance, and eloquence, they explain the Shari'a's laws and commands—not Islam's pillars of belief and elevated principles—in a simple, clear, and detailed language. In a unique, matchless style particular to the Qur'an, they usually end their explanations with a sentence or phrase related to belief, Divine Unity, or the Hereafter to make the Shari'a's laws universal and secure obedience to them through belief in God and the Hereafter.

To discover the elevated aspect of eloquence and what sorts of merits and subtleties are in the verses' conclusions, such as *God is All-Powerful over all things; God knows all things; He is All-Honorable, All-Wise; He is All-Honorable, Most Compassionate,* refer to the Second Ray of The Twenty-fifth Word's Second Light.

While explaining Islam's secondary principles and social laws, the Qur'an abruptly draws its audience's attention to elevated, universal truths, from the lesson of the Shari'a to the lesson of Divine Unity, and changes from a plain style to an elevated one. This shows that it is a book of law and wisdom, a book of creeds, belief, reflection, invocations, prayer, and call to the Divine Message.

By offering its aims of guidance on every occasion, the Qur'an's Madinan *sura*s display a brilliant miraculousness of eloquence and purity of language different from the styles of the Makkan *sura*s. Sometimes it uses two words, for example in the *Lord of the Worlds* and *your Lord,* to declare the manifestation of God's Names in all creatures and in one being, respectively. Doing so expresses the former within the latter. Some-times when it fixes an atom in the eye's pupil, it uses the same "hammer" to fix the sun in the heavens and make it an eye of the heavens.

For example, after beginning with: *He created the heavens and Earth,* the verse ends with: *He causes the night to enter into the day and the day to enter into the night; He has full knowledge of what is in the breasts* (57:4-6). This means: "Together with the magnificent creation and administration of Earth and the heavens, He has full knowledge of what occurs in the hearts." The simple style of speech aimed at ordinary people is manifested as an elevated and appealing address for the guidance of all.

**QUESTION:** Sometimes an important truth may remain hidden. Also, the reason for ending the narration of an ordinary event with a universal principle or a principle or aspect of Divine Unity cannot always be known. Some may consider this Qur'anic style defective. For example, after narrating how Joseph contrived to detain his brother (12:69-76), the Qur'an mentions an exalted principle: "Above every knowledgeable person is someone who knows more." This seems unrelated to the occasion with respect to eloquence. How do you explain this?

**ANSWER:** The Qur'an is a book of belief, reflection, and invocation, as well as a book of law, wisdom, and guidance. It therefore comprises, by its very nature, numerous books and contains innumerable instructions. To express the Divine Lordship's all-comprehensive and magnificent manifestations, it is a kind of copy and recitation of the great Book of the Universe. As a result, it pursues many aims in most of its long and medium-length *sura*s (each of which is like a small Qur'an), on each page, and in all its discussions.

Given this, the Qur'an gives instructions on every occasion in knowledge of God, aspects of Divine Unity, and truths of belief. Wherever a suitable occasion arises, no matter how insignificant it seems, the Qur'an gives other instructions, thus making that occasion significant and adding to its eloquence.

**QUESTION:** The Qur'an dwells too much on Divine Unity, the Hereafter, and God's Judgment of humanity, both explicitly and allusively. What is the Divine reason for this?

**ANSWER:** Consider this: The Qur'an was revealed to remove all doubt about the Divine control of Earth's changes, upheavals, and revolutions and in the universe's life, and to break the most obstinate resistance to confirming it. It also was revealed to instruct humanity, who shouldered the Supreme Trust and Earth's rule according to Divine laws, in the mightiest and most important aspects of its duties concerning eternal happiness or doom. If the Qur'an called attention to such matters even millions of times, it still would not be a waste of time or words, and they would be read and studied in the Qur'an millions of times without causing any boredom.

- From *Surat al-Buruj:*

> Those who believe and do righteous deeds, theirs will be Gardens underneath which rivers flow. (85:11)

This verse teaches that death, which always stands before us, is something that saves us, our world, and our beloveds from eternal execution, for it causes them to gain a magnificent, eternal life. Even if this verse were repeated billions of times, and if as much importance were attached to it as to the whole of existence, it still would not be excessive enough to devalue it.

In teaching countless, invaluable matters of this sort and trying to prove and establish in people's minds the awesome revolutions that will destroy and change the universe, the Qur'an constantly draws attention to those matters both explicitly or allusively. Since they are bounties like bread, air, light, and medicine, which we always need and that require renewal and refreshment, their reiterations are a Qur'anic grace.

• Consider the following:

For example, the Qur'an reiterates severely, angrily and emphatically such threatening verses as: *As for those who do not believe, for them is fire of Hell* (35:36), and *For wrongdoers is painful chastisement* (14:22). As discussed in the *Risale-i Nur*, humanity's unbelief is such a strong violation of the rights of most creatures that it angers

Earth and infuriates the elements. Thus they smite unbelievers with floods.

As explicitly stated in: *When they are flung therein (in Hell) they hear its roaring as it boils up, as if it would burst with rage* (67:7-8), Hell is so furious with unbelievers that it seems almost to burst with rage. If, in the face of such a comprehensive crime and a boundless aggression, and not from the perspective of physical insignificance but of the greatness of the unbeliever's wrongdoing and the awesomeness of unbelief, and in order to show the importance of His subjects' rights as well as unbelief's infinite ugliness and the deniers' iniquity, the Sovereign of the Universe has repeated in His Decree most angrily and severely such crimes and their punishments even billions of times, it still would not be a defect. That countless people have read these words every day for 1,400 years most eagerly and without boredom or lack of need demonstrates that it is not a defect.

Every day, for each person a world disappears and the door of a new world is opened. So, by repeating *There is no god but God* 1,000 times out of need and with longing to illuminate each of our transient worlds, we make each repetition a lamp for each changing scene. The Qur'an has various reasons for reiterating the Eternal Sovereign's threats and punishments, among them to break people's obduracy and free them from their rebellious carnal selves.

Thus it seeks to prevent them from darkening the changing scenes and ever-recruited worlds, disfiguring their images reflected in the mirror of their lives, and turning against them those fleeting scenes that probably will testify for them in the Hereafter. Even Satan does not consider the Qur'an's severe and forceful repetition of its threats as out of place. It demonstrates that the torments of Hell are pure justice for those who do not heed them.

- Consider the repetition of stories of the Prophets, particularly that of Moses:

Such stories contain many instances of wisdom and benefit. The Qur'an shows the Prophethood of all previous Prophets as an evidence of Muhammad's Messengership. This means that from the viewpoint of truth, no one can deny his Messengership unless one denies all other Prophets.

Also, since not everyone can recite the whole Qur'an at any time, it includes those stories, together with the essentials of belief, in almost all the long and medium-length *sura*s, thus making each one like a small Qur'an. Eloquence requires this, and it is done to show that Muhammad is the most important phenomenon of humanity and the mightiest matter of the universe.

The Qur'an gives the very highest position to the person of Muhammad and holds that he is God's Messenger, one of the two pillars of the affirmation of belief (which contains four essentials of belief) equal to the pillar *There is no god but God.* As the *Risale-i Nur* shows by means of it many proofs and signs, Muhammad's Messengership is the universe's greatest reality, his person is the most noble creature, and his universal collective personality and sacred rank (the Muhammadan Truth) is the brightest sun of both worlds. The *Risale-i Nur* also discusses the signs and evidences of his worthiness to occupy this extraordinary position. One of those thousands of evidences and signs is this:

According to the rule "the cause is like the doer," an amount of reward equal to the number of good deeds that his community has ever done or will do will be added to the Prophet's account. Since he illuminated all of the universe's realities with the light he brought, everything that exists is indebted to him and he incessantly receives the prayers and blessings of all creatures.

Furthermore, together with innumerable spirits, countless righteous members of his community have invoked God's peace and blessings on him for centuries, asking God to give him their spiritual reward and the merit of their prayers.

His record of good deeds also contains countless lights from his followers' recitation of the Qur'an, each letter of which results in as many as 10, 100, or 1,000 rewards. Knowing beforehand that the collective personality of that being (the Muhammadan Truth) would be like a blessed, elaborate tree of Paradise in the future, the Knower of the Unseen attached greatest importance to him in His Qur'an. In His Decree, He introduced the need for obeying him and of being honored with his intercession by following his way as the most important matters for humanity.

Thus, since the truths reiterated in the Qur'an have such a great value, anyone with a sound nature will testify that its repetitions contain a powerful and extensive miracle of meaning.

\*\*\*

**Two concluding notes**

**FIRST NOTE:** Twelve years ago, I heard that a dangerous and obstinate unbeliever ordered the Qur'an to be translated so that people could see its reiterations and understand just what it really is. He also intended to substitute the translation for the original in the prescribed prayers. However, as the *Risale-i Nur* shows decisively, an exact translation is impossible, for no other language can preserve Arabic's virtues and fine points, as Arabic is very strict in syntax and grammar. No translation can replace the Qur'an's miraculous phrases and words, which are comprehensive in meaning, and each letter of which brings from 10 to 1,000 merits.

The *Risale-i Nur* also stopped the plan to have only translations of the Qur'an recited in mosques. But since hypocrites taught by that heretic continue to seek a way to extinguish the sun of the Qur'an in the name of Satan, I felt compelled to write the Flower of Emirdag. As they do not allow me to meet with people, I have no knowledge of the latest developments.

**SECOND NOTE:** After our release from Denizli prison, I was sitting on the top floor of the well-known Hotel Sehir. The graceful dancing of the leaves, branches, and trunks of the poplar trees in the fine gardens opposite me, each with a rapturous motion like a circle of dervishes touched by a breeze, pained my heart, which was grievous and melancholy at being parted from the brothers and remaining alone.

Suddenly I recollected autumn and winter, and a heedlessness overcame me. I so pitied those graceful poplars and living creatures swaying with perfect joy that my eyes filled with tears. Since they reminded me of the separations and deaths beneath the universe's ornamented veil, the grief at a world full of death and separation pressed down on me.

Suddenly, the light of the Muhammadan Truth came and changed that grief and melancholy into joy. Indeed, I am eternally grateful to the person of Muhammad for the help and consolation that came to me at that time, for only a single instance of the boundless grace of that light for me, as for all believers and everyone. It was as follows:

Picturing those blessed and delicate creatures as trembling at death and separation, and going into non-existence in a fruitless season (the view of the heedless), weighed heavily on my feelings of passion for permanence, love of beauty, and compassion for fellow creatures and living things. It changed the world into a kind of hell, and the mind into an instrument of torture. Just at that point, the light that Muhammad brought as a gift for humanity lifted the veil and showed not extinction, non-existence, nothingness, futility, and separation, but meanings and purposes as numerous as the poplars' leaves, and, as demonstrated in the *Risale-i Nur*, results and duties that may be divided into certain types, as follows:

One type relates to the Majestic Maker's Names. For example, everyone applauds an engineer who makes an extraordinary machine: "What wonders God has willed. May God bless him (or her)." By carrying out its functions properly, the machine congratulates and applauds its engineer. Everything, every living creature, is such a machine and congratulates and applauds its Maker.

Another type of purpose for the lives of things like poplar trees is that they each resemble a text that, when studied, reveals knowledge of God to conscious living beings. Having left their meanings in such beings' minds, their forms in these beings' memories and on the tablets of the World of Symbols or Immaterial Forms, and on the records of the World of the Unseen and in the sphere of existence, they leave the material world for the World of the Unseen. In other words, they are stripped of apparent existence and gain many existences pertaining to meanings, the Unseen, and knowledge.

Since God's Existence and Knowledge encompass all things, there is no room in a believer's world for non-existence, eternal extinction, annihilation, and nothingness. But an unbeliever's world is full of non-existence, separation, and extinction. As a famous proverb states: "Everything exists for the one for whom God exists; nothing exists for the one for whom God does not exist."

In short, then, just as belief saves us from eternal punishment when we die, it saves everyone's particular world from the darkness of extinction and nothingness. Unbelief, especially denying God,

changes life's pleasure into painful poison, ter-
minates the individual and his or her particular
world with death, and casts such people into dark
Hell-like pits. Those who prefer this world over
the Hereafter should heed this. Let them find a
solution for this or accept belief, and save themselves from a fearful, eternal loss.

> Glory be to You. We have no knowledge save what
> You have taught us. You are the All-Knowing, the
> All-Wise.

Your brother who is in much need of your
prayers and misses you greatly.

— Said Nursi

# The Qur'an

### Nine points

**FIRST POINT:** Some people claim that the Qur'an's mysteries are unknown, and that its interpreters have not perceived its truths. This claim has two aspects, and those who make it fall into two groups. The first group comprises the people of truth and investigation. They say that the Qur'an is a boundless treasury and that all people, regardless of time, receive their share from its complementary, implicit truths (without interfering with the shares of others) after they acknowledge its principles and unchangeable commands.

The Qur'an becomes better understood over time and in more detail, and the dimensions of its meaning are clarified. However, this does not mean that we should doubt its literal, explicit truths expounded by our righteous predecessors, for belief in the certain and incontrovertible truths forming the fundamentals of the Qur'an and Islam is obligatory.

The Qur'an explicitly states that it was revealed in clear Arabic (in plain language) so that its meaning could be understood. The Divine address concentrates, reinforces, and elaborates on these meanings. Rejecting them means contradicting God Almighty and the Messenger's understanding. The explicit meanings forming the fundamental Qur'anic truths were derived from the source of Messengership and transmitted through established reliable channels. This cannot be doubted, for Ibn Jarir al-Tabari[42] related each verse's meaning to the source of Messengership through reliable chains of transmission, and wrote a comprehensive interpretation of the Qur'an.

The second group comprises either single-minded friends who make matters worse while trying to help, or devilish enemies who oppose Islam's commands and the truths of belief. They want to

---

[42] Al-Tabari (c839-923): Scholar and author of enormous compendiums of early Islamic history and Qur'anic exegesis. He condensed the vast wealth of exegetical and historical erudition of earlier Muslim scholars, and is renowned as a historian, *faqih* (jurist), and interpreter of the Qur'an. (Ed.)

make a way through the Qur'an's fortified *sura*s, which you say are like a steel citadel around the Qur'anic truths. They spread their false claims to cast doubt upon the truths of belief and the Qur'an.

**SECOND POINT:** God Almighty swears by many things in the Qur'an. There are numerous mysteries and subtle points in these oaths. For example: *By the sun and his morning brightness* (91:1), points to the truth expressed in The Eleventh Word and presents the universe as a palace or a city. *Ya Sin. By the Wise Qur'an* (36:1-2) reminds us that the Qur'an's miraculousness is so sacred that it is worth swearing by.

*By the star when it sets* (53:1) and: *No! I swear by the locations and fallings of the stars, a mighty oath if you but knew!* (56:75-76), point out that falling stars signal the banning of jinn and devils from hearing news of the Unseen. This ends any doubt about the Revelation's authenticity.[43] These oaths also remind us of the great power and perfect wisdom needed to establish the stars, those mighty heavenly objects, in their places in perfect

---

[43] In pre-Islamic times, mediums and seers tried to acquire limited news of the Unseen through jinn and devils. This door was closed when the Qur'an began to be revealed. (Ed.)

order, and in turning the planets with an amazing speed.

In oaths by angels responsible for winds: *By the scattering and winnowing* (51:1) and: *By the emissaries sent* (77:1), our attention is drawn to the significant wisdom in whirling winds and air waves. We are reminded that such supposedly "randomly moving" elements are, in fact, used for important services and subtle purposes.

In short, Qur'anic oaths contain many subtleties. As I have no time to explain all of them, I only point out one point in: *By the fig and the olive* (95:1).Through this oath, God Almighty reminds humanity of His Power's greatness, His Mercy's perfection, and His important bounties. This oath also points out that people heading toward the lowest rank can use thanksgiving, contemplation, belief, and good deeds to begin a spiritual evolution that eventually will allow them to reach the highest rank.

The fig and the olive are mentioned for a specific reason: These useful fruits contain many noteworthy subtleties. Olives are important in social and commercial life and are nutritionally rich. Figs are wonderful miracles of Divine Power (God encapsulates a huge fig tree within its sand-particle-sized seeds) that display many aspects of Divine Providence by lasting longer than most other fruits consumed by people. They also have many other beneficial properties that should be studied by scientists.

**THIRD POINT:** The abbreviated letters at the beginning of several Qur'anic *sura*s (*al-huruf al-muqatta'at*) are Divine ciphers through which God reveals some signs of the Unseen to His particular servant. The key is in the hand of that person and his heirs.

Since the Qur'an addresses every level of understanding in every age, all people, regardless of level and time, can comprehend it according to their level. The righteous predecessors had and disclosed the primary share. Saints and seekers of truth find therein many indications relevant to their spiritual journey toward the Unseen. In my *Isharat al-I'jaz* (Signs of Miraculousness), I explain those letters from the viewpoint of their miraculous eloquence at the beginning of *Surat al-Baqara*.

**FOURTH POINT:** The Twenty-fifth Word proves that a true and exact translation of the Qur'an is impossible. Its sublime style, an element of its miraculous meaning, cannot be imitated. Even explaining the truth and pleasure derived from its sublime style is impossible. However, I cite a few points to show the way to its understanding, as follows:

> And of His signs is the creation of the heavens and Earth and the variety of your tongues and colors. (30:22)

> And the heavens shall be rolled up in His Right Hand. (39:67)

> He creates you in your mothers' wombs, creation after creation in threefold shadows. (39:6)

> He created the heavens and Earth in 6 days. (7:54)

> God comes between a person and his own heart. (8:24)

> Not an atom's weight, or less than that or greater, escapes from Him in the heavens or in Earth. (34:3)

> He makes night pass into day, and makes day pass into night. He knows all that is in the breasts (hearts). (57:6)

In these verses, the Qur'an sublimely and miraculously portrays the truth of God's creativity. It shows that the universe's Builder puts all particles in their places, even in the eye's pupil, with the same instrument and at the same time as He fixes the sun and moon in their places. He makes and places the eyes and removes their veils according to the same measure and using the same immaterial instrument as that with which He uses to arrange and unfold the heavens. The Majestic Maker puts a person's unique facial features and outer and inner senses in their places with the same immaterial hammer used to fix the stars in the sky.

The verses also indicate that the Majestic Maker, in order to have the eyes see and the ears hear His acts while He is at work, uses the Qur'anic verses as a hammer to strike a particle and then strike the sun at the same time and with another word of the same verse. Such a sublime style shows Oneness in Unity, infinite Majesty within infinite Grace, boundless Might in utter secrecy, limitless extent in complete subtlety, infinite Grandeur within infinite Compassion, and endless distance in exact nearness. He demonstrates all opposites' ultimate unity. Although regarded as impossible, such a unity's existence is absolutely necessary for the universe's existence and life. Before such sublimity, the greatest literary figures can only prostrate in admiration.

The sublime Qur'an demonstrates the majesty and grandeur of His Lordship's Sovereignty through: *And of His signs is that the heaven and Earth stand firm by His Command; then, when He calls you once and suddenly out of the ground, you shall come forth* (30:25).

In other words, the heavens and Earth resemble the barracks or training grounds of magnificent armies. Lying behind the veils of non-existence and mortality, they appear in the Place of the Supreme Gathering with a perfect speed and in perfect obedience to a trumpet blast or the command: "Rise for the Last Judgment!"

This verse also refers to the universe's final destruction and the Resurrection in a miraculously exalted style, and to the following convincing proof: Seeds covered by and rotted away in the ground, as well as water evaporated and concealed in the atmosphere, reappear in this world every spring with perfect order and speed. This mimics the Resurrection, for the dead will be resurrected in the same way after the universe's final destruction.

Compare the degree of eloquence in other verses to those quoted above, and decide whether or not the Qur'an can be translated accurately in all its fullness. All that can be done, even as a first step, is to make a brief or a relatively long verse-by-verse interpretation.

**FIFTH POINT:** For example: *Al-hamdu li-llah* (All praise be to God) is a Qur'anic sentence meaning, according to Arabic syntax and semantics, that every praise and thanks that has been or ever will be uttered by any being is, in reality, for and deserved by the Necessarily Existent Being: God.

The meaning *every* derives from *al* (the). The meaning *by any being* derives from *hamd* (praise), for the original Arabic is in the infinitive form. Arabic expresses a general meaning by omitting the subject before an infinitive. As this sentence contains no object, although it is addressed to someone (or something) who is either present or absent, its meaning is general. Therefore, we derive *by any being* from this short sentence.

*That has been or ever will be* comes from the rule that transitioning from a verb clause to a noun clause indicates persistence and duration. *For and deserved by* are expressed in the preposition *li* (to or for God), which specifies and expresses deserving. Since *Allah* is the Divine Being's Greatest

Name, and since existence is essential and indispensable to the Divine Being and is a tableau to help reflect on the Majestic Being, *Allah* necessarily connotes the Necessarily Existent Being. If this is the explicit, briefest meaning of such a short sentence, which is agreed upon by linguists of Arabic, how can it be translated with the same strength and miraculousness?

Only one other language resembles Arabic in its syntax, but it cannot compete with Arabic in comprehensiveness. Given this, how can the Qur'an's sacred words, revealed in Arabic and therefore having a syntax and comprehensiveness displaying an All-Encompassing Knowledge penetrating everything at the same time, be translated into other languages with all of its subtle meanings, allusions, and miraculous style? In reality, each letter in the Qur'an is such a rich treasure of truths that its explanation could cover at least one page.

**SIXTH POINT:** To express this meaning better, I describe an event that enlightened me. Once I pondered over "we" in *You alone do we worship and You alone do we ask for help* (1:5), and tried to understand why *we* was preferred to *I*. The congregational prayer's merits suddenly dawned upon me, and I noticed that every member of the mosque's congregation was a kind of intercessor for me, a witness and supporter of the causes and truths I declare in my recitation. I felt encouraged to offer my faulty prayer to the Divine Court in the company of the congregation's comprehensive prayer. Another veil dropped, and I imagined all of Istanbul's mosques as one mosque, and their worshippers as one huge congregation. I felt included in their supplications and confirmations.

Afterwards, I imagined myself in the circular lines of worshippers around the Ka'ba, and said: "*Al-hamdu li-llah, Rabb al-'Alamin* (All praise be to God, Lord of the Worlds)," seeing that I had so many intercessors repeating and confirming every word of my prayer. This thought led me to see the Ka'ba as the prayer niche (*mihrab*). Entrusting to the blessed Black Stone my confession of faith: "I bear witness that there is no deity but God, and I bear witness that Muhammad is God's Messenger," which the whole congregation said, I saw that the congregation comprised three circles:

The first circle was the mightiest congregation formed by all believers and monotheists. The second circle was composed of all creatures engaged in a most comprehensive prayer and glorification of God, each species supplicating and praising in its own ways. Their services, called the "functions or duties of things," are the form of their worship. Aware of this, I said: "*Allahu akbar* (God is the greatest)" and bowed my head in wonder.

The third circle was my body, an amazing and yet seemingly slight and insignificant world, but in reality a very great and significant world due to the task it performs. Each part of it, from the cells to the outer senses, is busy with worshipping and giving thanks. In this circle, I felt the spiritual faculty in my heart reciting on that congregation's behalf: *You alone do we worship, and You alone do we ask for help*, as my tongue did on behalf of the other two congregations.

In sum, the *we* in *You alone do we worship* refers to those three congregations. Still in this state, I imagined that the spiritual personality of God's Messenger, the conveyor and transmitter of the Qur'an, assumed its grandest form in Madina, which could be regarded as his pulpit in this world, and was reciting: "O people, worship your Lord." I imagined the three congregations obeying him by reciting: *You alone do we worship*.

Then, according to the rule of "when something is established, it is established with all that is needed for it to be established," the following truth came to my mind: The Lord of the Worlds addresses all people and, through them, all creatures. God's Messenger then communicates that speech of honor to humanity, to all beings having spirit and consciousness, regardless of time. As the past and future thus can be regarded as the present, all people [regardless of time and place] listen to this address as a congregation composed of various lines.

This truth, however imaginal, showed me that each verse has a miraculous radiance in its subtle style, eloquence, and fluency. All of these come from the Eternal Speaker of Infinite Grandeur and Majesty through the illustrious transmitter who has the greatest rank of being beloved by God, and from the variety and multitude of its listeners. This makes the entire Qur'an, even each of its words, miraculous. I said: "All praise be to God for the light of belief and the Qur'an" and, emerging from the imaginal world I had entered through the letter *nun* (*n*),[44] understood that in addition to the Qur'an's

---

[44] *Nun* is prefixed and suffixed to a verb in different tenses to mean we, as in *na'budu* (we worship).

verses and words, even some of its letters, like the *n* in *na'budu*, are radiant keys to significant truths.

When my heart and imagination came out of this state, my reason said: "I want my share. I cannot fly like you. I walk on the feet of evidence and argument. You should show me the way to the Creator, the Worshipped One, Whose help is asked for, through *We worship* and *We ask for help* so that I can accompany you." In response, I told the heart to say to the bewildered reason:

> See how all creatures, whether animate or inanimate, worship God by doing their duties in perfect order and obedience. Some of them, despite being unconscious or dumb or unfeeling, perform duties in perfect order as if they were conscious and worshipping God. This means that the One, Truly Worshipped and Absolutely Commanding, employs them to worship Him.

> Look again, and see that all creatures, especially animate ones, have countless needs and demands that must be met if they are to exist and survive. They cannot meet even their most insignificant need on their own, and yet we see that their needs are met regularly, on time, and from an unexpected place.

Such infinite poverty and neediness, along with such an extraordinary satisfaction of their needs by the Unseen and the aid of Mercy, shows that they have an absolutely Rich, Generous, and Powerful Protector and Provider to Whom all things turn for help, especially living beings. In other words, through the language of asking for help, they say: You alone do we ask for help.

Reason responded: "I also believe and affirm."

**SEVENTH POINT:** Then I said: *Guide us to the Straight Path, the path of those whom You have blessed* (1:6-7). Immediately among all the caravans of humanity, I saw the illustrious caravan of the Prophets, truthful ones, martyrs, saints, and pious people pass into eternity along a straight highway, removing all darkness from the future. This supplication guided me to join that caravan. I suddenly said: "Glory be to God!" Anyone should be able to see what a great loss and perdition it is not to join that illustrious caravan progressing in utmost security to illuminate the future. Where can those who turn away by introducing un-Islamic innovations into Islam find light? What can they follow to salvation?

God's Messenger, who is our guide, declared: "Every innovation is a deviation, and every deviation leads to Fire."[45] What benefit do such evil scholars hope to gain? On what principle can they base their opposition to Islam's self-evident marks or public symbols or rituals (e.g., *adhan* [call to prayer], sacrificing animals on the Festive Day of Sacrifice, and Jumu'a and other congregational prayers)? How can they consider them changeable? They must be deluded by a transient, illusory light caused by an aspect of meaning.

For example, a peeled fruit may show its delicacy more clearly but all too briefly, for it is soon bruised and begins to rot. In the same way, the Prophetic and Divine expressions and concepts in Islam's public symbols or rituals are like a living and protecting skin. When removed, such as reciting the *adhan* in another language, its blessed meaning may seem brighter or more understandable. But it soon loses its freshness and spirit, leaving its "carcass" in dark minds and souls. Its light is extinguished, and only smoke remains.

**EIGHTH POINT:** The law has two spheres: individual rights and public law. Both are found in the Shari'a. This latter group, which can be regarded as

---

[45] Muslim, *Jum'a*, 43; Abu Dawud, *Sunna*, 5.

the rights of God, contains Islam's "public symbols or rituals" or "banners." Since all Muslims are concerned with these symbols, any interference without their consent transgresses their rights. Even minor symbols, like the commended duties, are just as important as Islam's most fundamental matters. Those who try to change or abolish these symbols, as well as their supporters, should understand that such matters concern all Muslims, for they are the radiant links joining all Muslims to Islam and each other since the Era of Happiness. They should understand that they are committing a most grievous sin. Anyone with even a bit of consciousness should tremble at the inevitable dire consequences.

NINTH POINT: Some Shari'a matters are related to worship. Being independent of human reason, the cause for their performance is God's command. Other Shari'a matters are the result of preferring a purpose or a comprehensible benefit. Nevertheless, the real cause for their legislation is the Divine command.

Public symbols related to worship cannot rely on any imagined or fancied benefit, regardless of the supposed beneficial results. No one can interfere with them. Also, the wisdom in or Divine purposes for their legislation or the resulting benefits are not restricted to their known benefits. For example, why does the *adhan* summon Muslims to prayer when firing a gun would achieve the same result? We should realize that the *adhan* has far more benefits than just this one. Firing a gun might achieve the same result, but how could it substitute for the *adhan*, which is also a means of declaring God's Unity on behalf of that area's people, the greatest purpose and result of creating humanity and the universe? It also expresses their servanthood and worship for Divine Lordship.

In short, there is a reason for Hell. Many things going on today make one want to shout: "Long live Hell!" Paradise does not come cheap, but rather at a very high price. Remember: *The inhabitants of the Fire and the inhabitants of Paradise are not equal. The inhabitants of Paradise—they are the triumphant* (59:20).

# Index